THE HOUND OF THE BASKERVILLES

Sir Arthur Conan Doyle

AUTHORED by Mae Ng
UPDATED AND REVISED by S.R. Cedars

COVER DESIGN by Table XI Partners LLC
COVER PHOTO by Olivia Verma and © 2005 GradeSaver, LLC

BOOK DESIGN by Table XI Partners LLC

Published by GradeSaver LLC, www.gradesaver.com

First published in the United States of America by GradeSaver LLC. 2013

ISBN 978-1-60259-410-4

Printed in the United States of America

For other products and additional information please visit
http://www.gradesaver.com

Table of Contents

Table of Contents

Biography of Doyle, Sir Arthur Conan (1859-1930)

Sir Arthur Conan Doyle, most famed for his four novels and fifty-six short stories about the "consulting detective" Sherlock Holmes, was born on May 22nd, 1859 in Edinburgh to a Catholic family of ten. His father, Charles Altamont Doyle, was an architect and an artist. Unfortunately, his talents were shadowed by alcoholism and epilepsy. He eventually died in an asylum where he was institutionalized. The family therefore suffered financially, though Doyle's mother, Mary, was able to pay for his schooling at a Jesuit institution.

Doyle decided to pursue medical studies at Edinburgh University, and had to take a job as a doctor's assistant to pay for his school fees. He was already writing and publishing stories by this time, but set up a practice in Southsea in the early 1880s. During this period, he completed the first Sherlock Holmes novel, *A Study in Scarlet*, which was published in *Beeton's Christmas Annual* in 1887. Sherlock Holmes was modeled after Doyle's university professor, Joseph Bell, whom he greatly admired. Doyle wrote to Bell, "It is most certainly to you that I owe Sherlock Holmes. ... [R]ound the centre of deduction and inference and observation which I have heard you inculcate I have tried to build up a man."

However, there was also much of Doyle himself in the character of Sherlock Holmes, as Bell himself once remarked. Doyle is known to have been analytical, attentive to detail, methodical (though occasionally absent-minded and clumsy), imaginative, and reserved. He even solved a mystery of a missing person in 1907 in only one hour's time. This case involved a countrywoman who was afraid that her cousin had been murdered; Doyle deduced from the man's bank records, however, that he had simply gone to Scotland.

In Doyle's two autobiographical works, *The Stark Munro Letters* and *Memories and Adventures*, he performed little analysis of either his own personality or spiritual problems. Like Holmes then, Doyle concealed his personal self. Similar to Holmes, Doyle was known as an energetic and prodigious person, who also would disappear into his study for days. As his son, Adrian, remarked: "My memories as a youth are mottled with sudden, silent periods when, following some agitated stranger, or missive, my father would disappear into his study for two or three days on end."

Doyle published other historical works as he endeavored to write serious, "better things." However, he took advantage of the up and coming *Strand Magazine* (1891) by publishing short stories there for financial gain. The Holmes short stories that he contributed became very popular with the reading public. The editor of the magazine, George Newnes, was committed to high-quality production and plenty of illustrations, including the memorable visual image of Sherlock Holmes designed by Sidney Paget.

The popularity of the Holmes stories secured Doyle financial comfort and fame, but he soon tired of his hero and "killed" him off in *The Final Problem* (1893). However, he later returned to stories about his hero when the public clamor proved too difficult to ignore. All the while, though, Doyle wrote other works and: took a post as a war correspondent in Egypt; supported the British management of the Boer War; oversaw a field hospital in South Africa; and was knighted in 1902. In 1902 Doyle penned one of his most famous Sherlock Holmes works: *The Hound of the Baskervilles*.

In 1912, Doyle wrote one of his other most enduring works, *The Lost World*. This science fiction tale centered on the character Professor Challenger's journey to the Amazon, where he discovers a place where dinosaurs and other prehistoric beasts still survive.

During World War I, Doyle became immensely interested in spiritualism, and he wrote many works on the subject. This new subject produced much criticism, especially regarding his support for the photographs of the Cottingley Fairies. Throughout this time, he continued to write poetry, short stories, pamphlets, and adventure novels. Some of his work dealt with humanitarian causes, an example being *The Crime of the Congo* (1909), which excoriated the brutality of the Belgians in the Congo.

Arthur Conan Doyle died on July 7th, 1930 of a heart attack; he was 71 years old. He was married twice; his first wife Louise died from tuberculosis in 1906, and his second wife Jean survived him. He had five children in total. He was buried in an anonymous grave in unconsecrated ground outside a churchyard fence, on account of his avowedly Spiritualist religious beliefs. The graveyard was later extended and now contains his grave. There are still no public headstones, however.

About The Hound of the Baskervilles

The Hound of the Baskervilles was written in 1901, eight years after Sir Arthur Conan Doyle had already 'killed off' Sherlock Holmes in his story, "The Final Problem." However, the novel was not a sequel - the events of *The Hound of the Baskervilles* take place before those of "The Final Problem."

When Doyle killed Sherlock Holmes, there was much public outrage and grief. More than twenty thousand people quit their subscription to the *Strand*, the magazine which had popularized the stories. After of *The Hound of the Baskervilles* proved such a great success, though, Doyle decided to bring the character back to life in 1903, with the story "The Adventure of the Empty House." Luckily, "The Final Problem" contained enough gaps that Doyle could plausibly claim that Sherlock Holmes had faked his own death.

The novel was published in serial form from 1901 to 1902, in the *Strand*. It is the third out of four novels which Doyle would write about Holmes. It continues to enjoy much success today, and is considered by some Sherlock Holmes scholars to be Doyle's best work. It has inspired over twenty film and television reinterpretations, made in places as diverse as Germany, Australia, the USSR, Canada, the United States, and of course, the United Kingdom. The most recent such reinvention of this story can be seen in the BBC series *Sherlock*, although this retelling very much differs from the original novel.

Doyle was inspired to write the novel after staying with his friend, Bertram Fletcher Robinson, in 1901. He named the character Sir Henry Baskerville after Robinson's gardener, named Harry Baskerville. Doyle had met Robinson on a return voyage from South Africa, and Robinson, a correspondent for the *Daily Express*, told him about a legend from his home region of Devon, England. Later, Doyle would write to his publisher that he felt he needed Robinson's name to appear next to his own. "I can answer for the yarn being all my own in my own style without dilution, since your readers like that. But he gave me the central idea and the local colour, and so I feel his name must appear," Doyle wrote.

Robinson showed Doyle the moor, know as Dartmooor, upon which the story is based. It is the largest open space in the southern region of England. In a letter to his mother, Mary, Doyle commented that the moor was "a great place, very sad & wild, dotted with the dwellings of prehistoric man, strange monoliths and huts and graves." The atmosphere of a place uninhabited by man is pervasive in the story, and marks a difference from many of Doyle's other Sherlock Holmes stories, insofar as it is set in the country rather than in London.

Character List

Holmes

Sherlock Holmes is the hero of this tale, and its most popular character. From other stories, readers would have known that Holmes is methodical, intelligent, analytical, observant, and reserved. In this novel, he also reveals his ability to match his brooding, thoughtful nature with immediate action. Willing to deceive or mislead others if necessary, Holmes is and antisocial and impersonal fellow who nevertheless comes off as charming and ultimately moral.

Watson

The narrator of the story and Holmes's closest friend, Dr. John Watson performs more of the detective work in *The Hound of the Baskervilles* that he does in many other Holmes stories. Though observant, Watson lacks Holmes's imagination and analytical ability. Without a doubt, he is firmly devoted to Holmes, and eager to please him. He is generally more sensitive to the feelings of others than Holmes is.

Dr. Mortimer

Dr. James Mortimer, the man who employs Holmes for this case, lives out on the moor and was a close friend of Sir Charles. Though a man of science (he is interested in the study of skulls), he somewhat accepts the legend of the hound because of a lack of evidence to the contrary.

Sir Charles

Sir Charles Baskerville is the figure whose death inspires the investigation. A nervous and philanthropic man, Sir Charles was well-loved amongst the moor population. He believed in the legend of the hound, a belief which his murderer used to scare him to death.

Hugo Baskerville

Hugo Baskerville is the long-deceased Baskerville whose treachery and wickedness supposedly inspired the curse of the Baskervilles. As the legend tells, he trapped a woman in his house, and then chased her when she escaped; he was in turn chased by a demonic hound that ripped his throat out and then haunted his descendants.

Sir Henry

Sir Henry Baskerville is the nephew of Sir Charles Baskerville, and heir of the Baskerville estate and fortune. He shows himself to be bold, practical and straightforward, but also impatient, hasty and stubborn. Though not initially superstitious, he later grows anxious over the legend.

Miss Stapleton

Miss Beryl Stapleton is the woman believed to be Stapleton's sister, but who is actually his wife. Though less wicked than he is, she has been his accomplice for a long time, having used the alias Mrs. Vandeleur. She tries to warn Sir Henry to flee the moor, but is unsuccessful partly because he falls in love with her.

Stapleton

Mr. Jack Stapleton, a "naturalist" who studies butterflies and plants out on the moor, presents himself as an eccentric but is actually the mystery's insidious villain. Born Rodger Baskerville, he has used several aliases in the past, including Mr. Vandeleur, and once managed a school. He is discovered to be a nephew of Sir Charles Baskerville, meaning he is therefore Sir Henry's cousin.

Cartwright

Cartwright is a boy who helps Holmes run detective errands. He not only helps Holmes with the investigation in London, but joins him out on the moor to bring him food and drink.

Barrymore

Mr. Barrymore is the butler of Baskerville Hall, and the man who discovered Sir Charles's body after he died. He and his wife have worked at Baskerville Hall for a long time. Though Barrymore seems secretive and sneaky, Watson discovers he is only employed in aiding his wife's brother Selden, and Barrymore ultimately provides crucial evidence to the investigation.

Mrs. Barrymore

Mrs. Barrymore is Barrymore's wife, and Selden's sister. Watson remarks that she seems to cry often.

Selden

Selden is a convict who has escaped to the moor from the nearby prison, Princetown. Mrs. Barrymore's younger brother, Selden is presented as a depraved creature beyond reform.

Frankland

Old Frankland is an old man who lives on the moor and enjoys causing legal trouble for his neighbors through frivolous lawsuits. A natural voyeur who uses his telescope to spy on others, he is also the miserly and indifferent father of Laura Lyons.

Laura Lyons

Laura Lyons is Old Frankland's daughter and Stapleton's mistress. Unhappily married to but separated from a cruel husband, she is promised help by Sir Charles, but then manipulated by Stapleton to help cause the former's death. She lives in Coombe Tracey, a town near the moor.

Lestrade

Lestrade is a police detective who comes to the moor when Holmes believes there is enough evidence available to arrest Jack Stapleton. He represents the official law, and frequently appears in Holmes stories.

Murphy

The only possible witness to Sir Charles's death, Murphy is a gipsy-horse dealer who lives out on the moor. He was drunk at the time of the murder, and can testify only to hearing cries.

Major Themes

Rationalism v. Superstition

One of the novel's primary themes is the conflict between rationalism and superstition. Much about the hound case suggest occult explanations, but Holmes steadfastly refuses to consider such possibilities. It is easy to understand why many turn to such explanations. It is not only that the people of the moor are primitive, tied to a folk religion. It is also that there is so little evidence with which to construct a rational explanation, other than the myth of the hound. Even a man of science - Dr. Mortimer - is driven to consider such occult possibilities.

But Holmes represents the power of the intellect: he possesses sound reasoning abilities and sharp observation skills. He tends to approach problems from a scientific standpoint, avoiding religion or superstition as causes. Instead of turning to implausible possibilities, Holmes seeks for clues where others have not looked. The idea seems to be that there is *always* a rational explanation; the evidence just might not always be easily observable. But the first step towards finding that evidence is to prize the power of the rational mind, and refuse to consider irrational possibilities.

Objects as Historical Artifacts

In many Sherlock Holmes adventures, objects play a significant role, since Holmes uses them to deduce truths not immediately observable to others. In *The Hound of the Baskervilles*, this theme is clear from the first chapter, in which Watson and Holmes each work to interpret Dr. Mortimer's walking stick. What Holmes illustrates is that every object has a history, which can be used to construct a story of its life. The larger implication of this approach is that humans *always* leave traces behind; one must simply know how to read those traces.

In context, this approach is particularly relevant since Scotland Yard (London's police) had recently begun using fingerprints in its criminal investigations. Obviously, the assumption with such technology is similar to Holmes's: people leave their unique marks everywhere. By learning to identify what is unique about an object (or the person who used it), one can eventually find a criminal from a crime scene.

The Holmesian methodology

Largely because of his singular detective method, Sherlock Holmes has remained a popular figure even today. That method is central to the story of *Baskervilles*. In interpreting it, one is lead to many questions: How does Holmes actually solve his cases? Is there a single method which he applies in all instances? Is it realistic? Is it replicable? Because he does not narrate the novel himself, Holmes does not exactly illustrate his approach to us, and we are left in large part to interpret it. There are two important elements to consider. The first is his method of observation, detailed in the "Objects as Historical Artifacts" theme section. The second is that Holmes considers multiple possibilities at once. Occasionally in this novel, he gives us an indication that he had to consider and then dismiss dead ends. Therefore, one could say that Holmes's approach is not as clean-cut as it seems at the end of the story, but instead is built of several guesses and false starts. In other words, it is arguably less scientific - making a hypothesis and then testing it - and more medical - diagnosing a problem by eliminating possibilities based on symptoms. No matter how one articulates the nature of Holmes's method, it remains one of the enduring themes of this novel and of Doyle's other Holmes stories.

Facts and Assumptions

Perhaps the greatest antagonist to Holmes's method is the human tendency towards assumptions. What most people do is study a scene in its entirety and then interpret its basic type. However, Holmes assumes nothing; he might identify the 'type' of scene he is studying, but then spends his energy looking for the particulars that make the scene unique.

The problem is that appearances can initially be deceptive, as a person might too quickly jump to conclusions. For example, Dr. Mortimer sees a paw print near Sir Charles's corpse, and concludes that there is truth to the hound legend. When Holmes instructs Watson to report *only* the facts of the moor, he is attempting to stop the man from integrating assumptions into his observations. Though this is almost impossible advice to follow - since Watson is naturally influenced by the atmosphere and his conjectures - he does use this understanding to conduct his own detective work, which yields dividends like the information about Laura Lyons. Holmes's suggestion seems to be that one must study the fact in itself, and then conduct guesswork based on it.

Urban life v. country life

The Hound of the Baskervilles explores on several occasions the distinctions between city and country lifestyles. In particular, one can observe the conflict in Watson himself. Whereas he is easily able to eschew supernatural explanations while in London, he finds himself more driven towards those possibilities when isolated in the country. Whereas the bustle of the city allows for a scientific approach, the atmosphere of the country dissuades it. In no uncertain terms, Watson calls the people of Devonshire primitive, and Baskerville Hall an evil place. Though certainly not a nuanced portrayal, Doyle's picture of country life is provocative and clear.

Moral, legal, and social order

The novel's story is largely contingent on the existence and legitimacy of established order. It is important to note that professional police forces did not exist in London until the 19th century. As the city grew, crime became more concentrated, and citizens needed better protection. Holmes takes the importance of such protection for granted. However, it is important to note that the law is rarely capable of the actual detective work in Holmes stories; that is certainly the case here. What drives Holmes, then, is a basic sense of morality. Even when he uses deceit, he does so for the ultimate good of catching the criminal. No matter which type of order Holmes employs, it is clear that he believes in the inherent value of such order.

Genius

Though it is hardly central to the story, the novel does explore the nature of genius. In particular, Holmes's attitude towards Watson suggests the idea that genius does not empathize with others. Not only does he use Watson as his pawn - sending him out to Devonshire as part of a ruse - but he also shows little sensitivity towards Watson's offense when he finds out. Instead, Holmes expects Watson to accept the intellectual necessity of that ruse. Holmes's lack of friends, his obsessive nature, and his general emotional distance all suggest that a true genius has little use for the trappings of ordinary life.

Glossary of Terms

almoner
chaplain or church officer who distributes alms

baying
prolonged howling

clandestine
secretive

craniology
the study of skulls

Dolichocephalic
a medical condition in which the head is longer than expected; Dr. Mortimer uses this term to describe Holmes' skull

dyspnoea
shortness of breath, caused by a cardiac disorder; this is believed to be the cause of Sir Charles's death

ferrule
a type of object used for fastening; used to describe part of Dr. Mortimer's walking stick

goyal
a deep trench, or ravine

guttering
flickering or low-lit, especially as regards a candle

M.R.C.S.
Membership of Royal College of Surgeons;Dr. Mortimer's was once a member of this organization

melancholy
a feeling of sadness

mire
a stretch of swampy ground

peremptory
insisting on immediate attention; brusque

quarry
a place from which stone has been excavated from the ground

skein
a length of thread or yarn; the phase is used metaphorically by Watson to describe the tangled case

tempestuous
characterized by strong and conflicting emotion

The Great Rebellion
refers to the Wars of the Three Kingsdoms, fought between England, Scotland and Ireland from 1639-1651; the reference in this novel helps date Hugo Baskerville's life

tor
a pile of high rocks, or a high rock

warder
a guard in prison

yew hedge
a tall bush which acts as a wall

Short Summary

This adventure concerns the mysterious death of Sir Charles Baskerville, and the possibility that the heir to his fortune might be the object of murder. Before the novel begins, Sir Charles Baskerville had died suddenly, perhaps the victim of a ghostly hound believed to haunt his family because of an age-old curse. The Baskerville estate is located out in the remote moor of Devonshire.

Holmes and Watson are introduced to the case by Dr. Mortimer, a friend of Sir Charles Baskerville. Mortimer believes that a hound has in fact killed Sir Charles, because he found a paw print near Sir Charles's corpse. He is worried that there may be some truth to the superstitious legend, which is detailed in an old manuscript, and thus approaches Holmes in hopes that the detective can protect Sir Henry, who is soon to arrive to claim the family estate and fortune.

When Sir Henry arrives in London, he exhibits no fear of the old legend. Instead, he insists on leaving soon for Baskerville Hall. However, several strange things happen while he is in London: an anonymous letter arrives, warning him to stay away from the moor; two boots are stolen from his hotel, each from a different pair; and Holmes observes a bearded man following him around the city. Certain that something insidious is afoot, Holmes sends Watson to Devonshire, where he is to accompany and protect Sir Henry while Holmes wraps up some business in London.

Upon his arrival in Baskerville Hall, Watson begins his detective work. He discovers several mysterious circumstances. There is an escaped convict, Selden, wandering the moor. Barrymore, the butler, frequently awakes in the middle of the night and shines a light from an empty room in the house. Mrs. Barrymore is constantly in tears.

Watson also meets the Stapletons, a brother and sister who are friendly neighbors of the Baskerville estate. However, Miss Stapleton is clearly anxious, since she secretly warns Watson to leave the moor immediately, before learning he is not actually Sir Henry.

Watson learns from Mr. Stapleton about the existence of Grimpen Mire, a part of the moor which is too dangerous to pass. On several occasions, he hears the frightening howl of a hound coming from this area of the moor.

One night, Watson and Sir Henry follow Barrymore, and discover that he and his wife are secretly feeding Selden, who is actually Mrs. Barrymore's brother. Watson and Sir Henry try to capture Selden, but fail. However, that night, Watson sees a mysterious figure standing alone up in the hills.

The next morning, the men promise Barrymore not to report Selden, and he in turn tells them how his wife found a letter that was sent to Sir Charles on the day he died.

Apparently, the man was outside that night to meet a woman with the initials L.L. Watson investigates to discover that this woman is Laura Lyons, who lives in the nearby Coombe Tracey. He visits her to learn that Sir Charles was going to give her money to secure a divorce, but that she did not keep her appointment that night because someone else offered her the money.

Watson then tries to track down the mysterious man on the moor, and discovers that it is actually Sherlock Holmes, who has been living secretly on the moor to observe the mystery from a distance. He explains that his open presence would have compromised his investigation. While there, Holmes has learned that Mr. Stapleton is in fact married to Miss Stapleton; they are not brother and sister, but have instead assumed fake identities. He believes Stapleton is responsible for Sir Charles's death, but he does not have the proof yet.

Suddenly, Watson and Holmes hear the same cry Watson heard earlier, and they rush to find a corpse out on the moor. Though they initially believe it is Sir Henry's body - since the figure is dressed in the man's clothes - they soon discover it is actually Selden's corpse. He had clearly been fleeing something, and had fallen from a cliff in the process. As they debate what to do with the body, Stapleton arrives. Though surprised, he quickly recovers his composure and easily identifies Sherlock Holmes.

Holmes accompanies Watson to Baskerville Hall, and has dinner with Sir Henry. During dinner, they learn that Stapleton had invited Sir Henry to dinner, and hence had been expecting him, not Selden, to be out on the moor that night. Selden was dressed in Sir Henry's clothes because Barrymore had given them to the convict.

Holmes notices a portrait of Hugo Baskerville, and secretly indicates to Watson that the face bears a striking similarity to Stapleton's. He thereby realizes that Stapleton must be a Baskerville, who hopes to kill off the surviving family members so that he will inherit the fortune.

However, Holmes does not tell Sir Henry the truth. Instead, he claims that he and Watson are returning to London, and instructs Sir Henry to join Stapleton for dinner the following night. Though it requires him walking alone across the moor, Sir Henry agrees.

That night, Holmes, Watson, and the London policeman Lestrade - who joined Holmes via train - stake out Stapleton's house. Watson sneaks close to spy Stapleton dining alone with Sir Henry; Miss Stapleton is absent. A fog compromises visibility, so the party has to retreat a bit. It is from this vantage that they soon see Sir Henry stroll past, and then a savage hound, flames seemingly leaping from its mouth, fly after the man. They are able to kill it only with several shots, right before it is prepared to rip out Sir Henry's throat.

Holmes studies the hound's corpse to discover that its mouth has been lined with phosphorus, thereby creating the image of flames, and its fur covered with a glitter.

They try to pursue Stapleton, but only find Miss Stapleton, who has been tied up, gagged, and locked away in the house. She tells them that Stapleton had restrained her, and likely fled out into Grimpen Mire, which is where he kept the hound locked away.

The next morning, they search Grimpen Mire, but find only Stapleton's boot. They assume he has died. They also find evidence of where he kept the hound, and that Stapleton had been feeding the beast with other animals.

A month later, Sir Henry and Dr. Mortimer embark on a trip around the world, so that Sir Henry can recover from his shock. One day, Watson questions Holmes about the case, and the detective provides all the missing pieces. Stapleton's actual name was Rodger Baskerville; he is the son of Sir Charles's youngest brother, who had long before moved to South America. After his father's death, Stapleton fled to England, changed his identity, and set out to construct a means to claim the Baskerville fortune. His wife had eventually tried to stop him, which is why he locked her away.

The details provided, Holmes invites Watson to join him for dinner and a show.

Quotes and Analysis

"If I have set it down it is because that which is clearly known hath less terror than that which is but hinted at and guessed at."

The Baskerville manuscript, p. 149

This quotation is from the 1742 manuscript that details the legend of the hound, and it gives the document an air of authority. The manuscript seems to provide the best explanation for the mysterious events which occur in the novel - if one allows a religious world view. Though it does provide a basis to explain Sir Charles's death, it is important to remember that the manuscript is 150 years old, even at the time of the novel's events. It reflects an attitude that accepts superstition as fact. For Holmes, the fact that the legend is "written down" does not at all make it "clearly known." Instead, this professed authority is just an example of the type of assumption that hinders true investigation. The contrast between the manuscript's professed authority and the actual explanation shows how knowledge had changed in the 18th century. It also reveals the human tendency to accept occult explanations when others do not easily present themselves.

"I knew that seclusion and solitude were very necessary for my friend in those hours of intense mental concentration during which he weighed every particle of evidence, constructed alternative theories, balanced one against the other, and made up his mind as to which points were essential and which immaterial."

Watson, p. 162

Here, Watson provides one of his clearest understandings of Holmes's method. Though he is the detective's partner, Watson is often left out of the man's problem-solving. Here, Watson implicitly defends Holmes's distance, suggesting that genius needs solitude. By suggesting that Holmes uses a method that Watson cannot replicate, Watson paints Holmes as not only a genius but as a hero. It also reflects the self-sufficiency that Holmes employs throughout the mystery, using others only when he needs them. Amusingly, one can claim that Watson is essential towards allowing Holmes the illusion of self-sufficiency (in other words, Holmes without Watson could not get as far), but the quote in any case gives some indication into how Watson - and Doyle - understand genius.

"The world is full of obvious things which nobody by any chance ever observes. Where do you think that I have been?"

Holmes, p. 163

When Holmes addresses Watson this way after Watson returns from his club, the detective gives some great insight into his method. In short, he is capable of observing and managing many details at once, so that he can often do his best work from the comfort of his armchair. And yet that observation is only the first step - what he can do afterwards is construct many possible interpretations for each observation at once. His true gift is for imaginative recreation. Therefore, what he suggests here is that can 'travel' to many myriad places simply in the confines of his imagination.

"Of course, if Dr. Mortimer's surmise should be correct, and we are dealing with forces outside the ordinary laws of Nature, there is an end of our investigation. But we are bound to exhaust all other hypotheses before falling back upon this one."

Holmes, p. 164

Though somewhat disingenuous here - Holmes would likely never accept an occult explanation for anything - he does illustrate what fascinates him most: cases which seem to have no explanation. This is because such cases allow Holmes the opportunity to employ his method, of observing the tiniest details and then constructing an explanation from them. When nobody else can see clues in a situation, then Holmes enjoys himself most of all, both because it allows him to display his genius and because it poses the challenge of exploring several different "hypotheses."

"But we hold several threads in our hands, and the odds are that one or other of them guides us to the truth. We may waste time in following the wrong one, but sooner or later we must come upon the right."

Holmes, p. 181

After Holmes and Watson encounter several dead ends in their investigation, it is notable that Holmes does not panic. Instead, he seems almost enthralled by the multitude of "threads." His faith that one of these threads will lead to the solution is built upon his basic belief that humans always leave a trail. He knows he will eventually find the right clues, and so seems to enjoy when that proves difficult. Finally, his confidence is not only in himself, but in the power of the intellect. Because he can eschew the possibility of occult explanations, he knows a rational solution will eventually be found.

"Just tell me what it all means, Watson, and I'll owe you more than ever I can hope to pay."

Sir Henry, p. 231

When Sir Henry addresses Watson this way, asking why Stapleton would so vehemently oppose the man's union with Miss Stapleton, it provides the latter the rare opportunity to play the primary detective, both for his charge and for us as readers. Typically in Holmes stories, Watson asks Holmes the explain the situation; here, Watson is the one being asked that question. This alternate situation describes the whole middle of the novel, when Watson is (seemingly) alone with Sir Henry out on the moor. Watson's means of attempting to answer questions like this provide a wonderful foil to Holmes's method, which usually drives the stories and which certainly drives the latter section of this novel. Finally, this moment employs situational irony, since Sir Henry is actually asking the question that could unravel the whole mystery, even though he believes he is only asking a question about romance.

"A spectral hound which leaves material footmarks and fills the air with its howling is surely not to be thought of. Stapleton may fall in with such a superstition, and Mortimer also; but if I have one quality upon earth it is common sense, and nothing will persuade me to believe in such a thing."

Watson, p. 245

When Watson records this passage in his diary, he has been away from Holmes for some time. What this passage reflects is the human tendency to turn to occult or supernatural explanations when no rational evidence presents itself. Even Watson - who vehemently insists that he will consider no occult explanations - exhibits that tendency here. By having Watson battle this tendency, Doyle explores the conflict between the rational and supernatural, and provides an extra hurdle that Holmes has to conquer. Watson speaks as though he must fight his instincts in order to pursue a rational course; it is often easier to settle for an occult explanation, which is why it is all the more important that we insist to ourselves that such explanations are impossible.

"Always there was this feeling of an unseen force, a fine net drawn round us with infinite skill and delicacy, holding us so lightly that it was only at some supreme moment that one realized that one was indeed entangled in its meshes."

Watson, p. 267

Here, Watson describes his feelings as he approaches the hut where the mysterious figure seems to be living. Of course, he soon discovers that it is Holmes himself who has drawn this "net" around him. The net is an important image in the novel, symbolizing the way knowledge is used to manipulate others like puppets or toys. Those who possess knowledge control those who do not have it. For example, Stapleton orchestrates Sir Charles's death and creates an aura of superstition because he knows much that others on the moor do not. Similarly, Holmes must hoard his own knowledge throughout the case, so that Stapleton does not realize that they are on his trail. Only when knowledge is kept secret or private can it become a "net," a means of control.

"I shall soon be in the position of being able to put into a single connected narrative one of the most singular and sensational crimes of modern times."

Holmes, p. 294

Holmes confidently announces this prediction even before he has entirely solved the crime. In fact, he must have Stapleton re-enact a version of the original crime in order to catch the culprit red-handed. Holmes's confidence in those circumstances reveals his belief that any trail will eventually lead to its end; he does not need to have the answer, but only needs to know he has chosen the right path out of all the possible paths. Then, trusting his power of observation, he knows that the markers humans leave behind will eventually reveal the final solution. The quote also reminds us that Holmes likes difficult cases most of all; "singularity" is an essential quality in a case that interests Holmes. In nearly every one of his cases, he remarks on the uniqueness of its clues.

"One of Sherlock Holmes' defects--if indeed, one may call it a defect--was that he was exceedingly loath to communicate his full plans to any other person until the instant of their fulfillment. Partly it came no doubt from his own masterful nature, which loved to dominate and surprise those who were around him. Partly also from his professional caution, which urged him never to take any chances. The result, however, was very trying for those who were acting as his agents and assistants."

Watson, p. 295

Watson writes this right before he reveals everything that Holmes told him about the case. The passage tells a lot about Holmes's personal character: the man is often uncommunicative, distant, and "trying" (or annoying). Of course, Watson suggests that there are contradictory reasons for his silence. On the one hand, he is extremely self-sufficient, and likes to maintain control of a situation. This is likely the "trying" aspect, since it is solely about Holmes's ego. On the other hand, Watson *does* recognize value in secrecy, since its allows Holmes to manipulate situations, to avoid "chances" that indiscriminate sharing might produce. Ultimately, Watson's feelings about Holmes are ones we likely feel as well. *The Hound of the Baskervilles* leaves out much of Holmes's thought process, so that we often lack even the information with which Holmes constructs his theories. Like Watson, we must simply wait to learn the fruits of that method when Holmes is ready to share.

Summary and Analysis of Chapters I-II

Summary

Chapter I: Mr. Sherlock Holmes

Watson walks into Holmes's breakfast-room, where Sherlock Holmes is having breakfast. Watson examines a walking stick which a visitor, James Mortimer, had left behind the night before, after finding nobody there to receive him. Mortimer's name is engraved into the stick.

Though his back is turned to Watson, Holmes sees his friend through the reflection in his coffee-pot. He surprises Watson by addressing him, and then asks him to deduce the character of James Mortimer from his stick.

Based on the stick, Watson believes that Dr. Mortimer is an elderly, well-respected doctor who lives in the country. He further deduces that Mortimer has received this stick as a gift from a hunting club.

Holmes initially compliments Watson's detective skills, but then clarifies that he is only complimenting the way that Watson has stimulated his own thought process. Holmes examines the stick himself, and concludes that Mortimer received the stick as a gift from a hospital, rather than from a hunting club. He deduces that Mortimer was a student at this hospital, not a physician, and that he must therefore be young, not old. Further, he believes that Mortimer has withdrawn from a town hospital to begin his own practice in the country. He adds that Mortimer must be absent-minded, amiable, unambitious and a dog owner.

Astonished, Watson looks in his Medical Dictionary for public information about Mortimer. The book confirms that Mortimer is a young man who studied as Charing Cross Hospital. Holmes begins to explain how he deduced that Mortimer owned a dog, but sees a dog from his window and realizes that Dr. Mortimer has now returned to pay them a visit.

Dr. Mortimer enters, and Watson describes him as a tall, thin man with bad posture, and dressed in a messy manner. Relieved that he left the stick there and did not lose it, Dr. Mortimer reveals that he received it not on the occasion of leaving Charing Cross, but for his wedding.

First, Dr. Mortimer notes that he had heard of Holmes through his reputation for solving difficult problems. Strangely, Dr. Mortimer then compliments the shape of Holmes's skull, and tells him that it would be an "ornament to any anthropological museum" (143). He explains that he studies skull shapes.

Holmes asks why Dr. Mortimer has called on him, and Mortimer tells him that he has a most serious and extraordinary problem.

Chapter II: The Curse of the Baskervilles

Dr. Mortimer explains that he has brought a manuscript, but Holmes has already observed it in his pocket, and surmises aloud that it is from the early eighteenth century. Confirming that observation, Dr. Mortimer explains that the manuscript was given to him by Sir Charles Baskerville, a close friend who had died three months earlier. Dr. Mortimer lives in Devonshire, which is out in the moor of England, and near the Baskerville estate.

To best explain his purpose, Dr. Mortimer first reads the document, which details a legend about the Baskerville family. The writer of the story identifies himself as a Baskerville, and explains that this legend has been passed down in his family over several generations. During the Great Rebellion (around the mid-1600s), the Baskerville estate was owned by Hugo Baskerville, a "wild, profane, and godless man" (146). When one young woman refused to return his advances, he trapped her an upper chamber of his house. She escaped one night while Hugo was entertaining friends, and Hugo declared that he would give his body and soul to "the Powers of Evil" if he could find her (147). One man suggested that they set the hounds after her, and Hugo took his advice before chasing her out into the moor on his black mare.

Thirteen men followed Hugo, who was ahead of them. They encountered a shepherd who was "crazed with fear" - he had seen the maiden, but had also seen a "hound of hell" in fast pursuit of Hugo (148). Eventually, the men encountered Hugo's mare, alone and frothing at the mouth. Frightened, they persevered until they came across a trench, next to which the hounds were whimpering. In the trench, three of the men found the maiden, dead "of fear and of fatigue", and Hugo, dwarfed by a "great, black beast, shaped like a hound" (148). The giant hound tore Baskerville's throat out, at which point the men fled. One of the men died that night, while the other two remained "broken men" for the rest of their days (149).

The writer concludes his story by insisting that the hound has plagued the Baskerville family even since, and warns his sons to never cross the moor at night.

After finishing the letter, Dr. Mortimer is surprised to see Holmes yawn; he thinks the tale is only interesting to a "collector of fairytales" (149). Dr. Mortimer then gives Holmes a newspaper clipping detailing Sir Charles Baskerville's recent death.

The newspaper story first describes Sir Charles Baskerville. At the time a probable candidate for the upcoming election, Baskerville had earned his fortune from South African speculation, and lived childless in the countryside, where he was involved in much philanthropy. The story then explains the circumstances of his death. When Sir Charles did not return from his usual nightly walk down an alley of trees behind

Baskerville Hall, his servant Barrymore investigated to find his body. The mystery was increased because there were no signs of violence on his body, and because his footprints suggested he had been walking on his tip-toes. One witness, a gypsy horse-dealer named Murphy, had heard cries but admitted he was drunk. Authorities concluded that Sir Charles had died from cardiac exhaustion, ruling out any suggestions of mystical stories. Finally, the article identifies his next of kin as his nephew, Mr. Henry Baskerville, who is supposedly in America.

More interested now, Holmes asks Dr. Mortimer for details not included in the article. Though he considers himself a man of science, Dr. Mortimer admits he has some strange suspicions. He considered Sir Charles a close friend, since they were two of the few intellectuals living out on the moor. The only other men of note are Stapleton and Mr. Frankland.

In the days before the man's death, Dr. Mortimer noticed that Sir Charles was growing anxious over the legends of the hound. One night, after seeing a black shape cross their paths, Sir Charles admitted his fears, and Dr. Mortimer convinced him to escape to London. He died the night before he planned to leave. Finally, Dr. Mortimer adds that upon investigating the scene of Sir Charles's death, he found the footprints of a gigantic hound. He did not reveal this information to the press.

Analysis

Readers of this time would have been quite familiar with the Holmes and Watson dynamic - Holmes is always able to outdo Watson with his genius, though the latter constantly works to impress his mentor. Therefore, the novel's opening would be immediately enjoyable for Doyle's readers. In the first chapter, Holmes seems to be testing Watson. There are several reasons why this is important. First, Watson is a smart, medical man capable of sound reasoning, an admirable thinker. The fact that his abilities are nevertheless dwarfed by Holmes's method is confirmation that Holmes possesses a unique, unmatchable genius.

And yet Watson is a crucial part of the dynamic, since he is the storyteller. It is notable that nearly all of Sherlock Holmes's tales are told by Watson, not just in *Hound* but in Doyle's ouvre overall. Watson's first-person addresses are useful for several reasons. First, they allow him to parcel out the information, so that the reader can try to piece together evidence himself, to get ahead of the case. Because Watson is usually behind Holmes, he is able to replicate that experience for the reader. So when Holmes reveals his own line of reasoning, usually after Watson's attempts, the reader gets to enjoy the solution more personally.

And yet Holmes's line of reasoning usually employs details that Watson does not record. The implication is clear: detective work is performed first and foremost by looking. Holmes's approach touches on an underlying belief of the work: that humans leave traces and evidence, wherever they go. The object in the first chapter, the walking stick, tells a story because the human who owns it has left traces on it.

History is always able to be pieced together from physical evidence. Again, the detective succeeds not because he knows something we do not, but because he knows how to look.

Further, from a storytelling perspective, Holmes's narration would undoubtedly be too tedious to record. Because he is capable of holding many possibilities in his head at once, many of which he considers only in order to disprove, his storytelling would lack the narrative thrust of Watson's. Therefore, Watson serves an economic function in the narrative: he observes just enough detail for the reader to understand the intricacies of a case, but he does not observe everything that Holmes does.

In this case, Holmes is shown to be fallible when he cannot deduce every detail about Dr. Mortimer's life from his walking stick. For example, he is surprised to hear that Mortimer received the stick as a gift for his wedding. Such fallibility in the first chapter is important towards making Holmes's powers believable. In other words, he does not have a telepathic gift. This is important because the world depicted in the detective story is always able to be explained through the intellect, rather than through divine or supernatural causes. There is no need for religious belief, a fact which plays directly into the Baskerville case.

Much about the case is intriguing for the reader, though, because it *does* imply a supernatural quality. Even though the characters have not yet traveled to the moor, it is painted in evocative strokes here, as it often was in English literature, as a dark, gloomy place where spirits might wander. There is an immediate atmosphere established, which is part of what makes this novel so popular amongst the Holmes stories.

For Holmes, such atmosphere is irrelevant, however, compared to the evidence. What is initially puzzling is that the evidence - the manuscript, a newspaper clipping, and Mortimer's own observations - together suggests an occult mystery because the clues do not connect to any rational explanation. The legend has even managed to convince a man of science, Dr. Mortimer, that an evil hound might be lurking the moor. Therefore, there is a contrast between science and occult beliefs. While men of intelligence want to believe in science, they understandably turn to superstition when they cannot explain something. So before he even gets involved in the case's particulars, Holmes faces a bigger question: is science capable of explaining even that which appears to defy explanation?

Summary and Analysis of Chapter III-IV

Summary

Chapter III: The Problem

Dr. Mortimer explains that the footprints were found 20 yards from the body, and that he would likely have overlooked them had it not been for the legend.

Holmes then questions him, asking for details about the alley where Sir Charles died. As Dr. Mortimer explains, it consists of a gravel path surrounded by tall hedges on two sides. One part of the alley leads to a summer house; the other end leads to the main house. One hedge is interrupted by a wicket-gate, which opens out onto the moor. Hence, there are three entrances to the alley overall. Finally, he notes that the main alley path is separated from the hedges by strips of grass.

Holmes is upset that Mortimer did not call him immediately, since clues have obviously been erased in the interim. Mortimer counters that the case might be beyond Holmes's abilities, since it features supernatural elements. According to reports, several people had seen an unnatural creature on the moor, even before Sir Charles died. No such reports have been filed since the death. Holmes then questions why Mortimer would include him at all, and Mortimer explains that Sir Charles's nephew and the next heir, Sir Henry Baskerville, is to arrive in London, and Dr. Mortimer is worried for his safety. He believes that it is important for the moor community to keep a resident in Baskerville Hall, one who can continue Sir Charles's philanthropy, or he would otherwise simply warn Sir Henry away.

Holmes advises Dr. Mortimer to meet Sir Henry at Waterloo as they had planned, and to mention nothing about the hound. He further instructs Mortimer to bring Sir Henry to him on the next morning, by which point Holmes will have determined the proper course of action.

After Dr. Mortimer leaves, Watson leaves Holmes alone to think. When Watson returns later, he finds the room filled with tobacco smoke. With little effort, Holmes perceives that Watson has spent all day at his club. He then shows Watson a map which he has obtained of the moor, and points out the various locations mentioned by both Dr. Mortimer and the manuscript author.

Holmes proposes that there are two questions before them: first, has any crime been committed at all? And second, what is the crime and how was it committed?

Watson finds the case bewildering; Holmes agrees that it has a "character of its own" (164). He believes the tip-toe footprints are signs that Sir Charles was running, though he does not know what the man was fleeing. The fact that he ran away from the house rather than towards it suggests he was terrified out of his wits. Holmes also believes that Sir Charles must have been waiting outside for someone, which would explain the cigar ash that Dr. Mortimer described.

Chapter IV: Sir Henry Baskerville

The next morning, Dr. Mortimer and Sir Henry arrive, with a brand new mystery. Someone has sent a letter to his hotel, constructed of printed words cut from somewhere and then pasted. It reads: "As you value your life or your reason keep away from the moor" (167). Only the word "moor" has been hand-written. The mystery is all the more disconcerting since nobody knew which hotel Sir Henry planned to stay at.

From the typescript, Holmes quickly discerns not only which newspaper the words were taken from, but also from which article, and in fact determines that the words were cut with nail scissors. He further deduces that the person who composed this letter was educated, but wished to pose as an uneducated man. He suspects the culprit worried that Sir Henry would either recognize his handwriting or soon enough encounter it. Finally, he notes that the letter's composer was in a hurry, likely because he feared an interruption.

Holmes asks Sir Henry if anything else of interest has happened to him. Though shocked at this turn of events, the man explains that one of his brand new boots is missing after he left them in the hotel hallway to be polished.

Sir Henry demands to know what is happening, so Dr. Mortimer tells his story. Intrigued, Sir Henry admits he has heard the legend but never taken it seriously. When Holmes follows with his belief that there is some danger at Baskerville Hall, Sir Henry angrily declares that there is "no man upon earth who can prevent me from going to the home of my own people" (174). However, he invites Holmes to lunch later that day, at which point he will have though the matter through.

As soon as Sir Henry and Dr. Mortimer leave, Holmes jumps to action. He and Watson follow the men, and notice another man following them from a cab. Watson notes that this man has a bushy black beard and a pair of piercing eyes. When the cab suddenly rushes off, Holmes attempts to hail his own cab, but fails. Cursing his bad luck, Holmes admires the culprit's cleverness, but is glad he was able to note the cab number before it left.

Holmes asks Watson to summon a boy named Cartwright, whom Holmes then orders to check the waste baskets of all the nearby hotels, in search of the newspaper that was used to construct the note. Once Cartwright leaves, Holmes plans to send an inquiry after whomever the cab driver was.

Analysis

In Chapter III, Dr. Mortimer presents his own interpretation of the facts, thereby leaving Holmes to begin his investigation. For most readers - of Doyle's day and today - this is where the fun begins. And yet, significantly, the gap between Holmes's thought process and what the reader hears is quite large. We do not know what theories Holmes may be entertaining about the case: does he believe in the existence of the dog? Does he think that someone murdered Sir Charles, even though the medical evidence suggests a natural death? Does he believe that someone will murder Sir Henry too? We are only left to understand that Holmes must undergo a long process of solitary reasoning before he shares anything with Watson (and by extension, us).

The question then becomes: what does the reader know about Holmes' method of "deduction"? Is it really scientific? Can we really believe in Holmes's genius? As we work to determine our own theories based on Dr. Mortimer's facts, we also anticipate what alternate approach Holmes will eventually use.

One indication of Holmes's process that is present in Chapter III is his attention to details. What Holmes sees is how various clues are connected to each other. In particular, he is intrigued by the clues which cannot be accounted for. As example, he is most taken by the existence of the "tip-toe" footprints (164). Already, this is his entry point into the case.

However, it is important to note that Holmes is not simply interested in the unexplainable. In other words, he is not intrigued by the suggestion of myth, which would explain the mystery through occult means. Because he refuses to consider that the footprints have a supernatural element, he is able to deduce that Sir Charles was not tip-toeing, but was instead fleeing something. Because he assumes that everything has a rational explanation, he is able to transcend the more simplistic, occult explanations that Dr. Mortimer seems to take for granted.

Holmes's treatment of clues is even more poignant in Chapter IV. His process here indicates his basic approach: he uses an understanding of types - a classification system - to explain the meaning of a particular clue. First, we see his familiarity with typescripts: he can identify to what medium a particular clipping belongs based off of its type. He then follows the trail to deduce the type of person who would read this kind of newspaper.

His next step is to ask Sir Henry if anything else strange has happened. Naturally, Sir Henry did not think enough of the boot to mention it on his own; such small events happen to us all the time. However, Holmes knows that the devil is in the details, that the answer is often in the places we otherwise think meaningless. Instead of judging the boot incident as trivial (as Dr. Mortimer does), Holmes wishes to methodically compare the ordinary to the unusual. In other words, the usual type (both boots remain) is compared to a specific instance (one boot is missing), to determine the reality of the situation.

Put another way, Holmes's method involves using general types to analyze specific incidents. This approach mirrors the scientific theories of Doyle's day, which classified various animal and plant species according to their types. In this way, understanding the class to which something belongs can help Holmes understand more about a particular entity. At the same time, understanding how something differs from its general class allows the observer to determine what specifics comprise clues worthy of consideration.

Chapter IV is notable too because it shows Holmes transitioning from a man of thought to a man of action. While he is able to deduce much from the past, he does not know where his future action will lead. And yet he is equally excited to follow the trail. This reveals another of his methods: he must facilitate the creation of clues, and not simply wait until they come to him. The mystery is very much alive, and he wishes to act as catalyst towards its unfolding.

From this perspective, decisions are extremely important, as they affect how the mystery unfolds. It is notable that Holmes criticizes himself as having approached the situation incorrectly. He regrets that his over-eagerness apprises the bearded man of their suspicions. The active trail must be treated with care if it is to lead to more evidence, meaning that Holmes's brilliance must extend not only to analysis, but to decision-making.

Finally, it is interesting that Holmes acknowledges his adversary's cleverness. For the story to be interesting, the pursued person (here, the man in the cab) must be a match for Holmes. Such a match of intellect is crucial not only for the reader - who wants an interesting story - but also for Holmes himself - who would likely be bored if he did not confront a mystery worthy of his genius.

Summary and Analysis of Chapter V

Summary

Chapter V: Three Broken Threads

After two hours in a museum - Watson remarks on Holmes's unique ability to divert his attention when necessary - they visit the Northumberland Hotel, where Sir Henry Baskerville is staying. Examining the register, Holmes pretends to know two of the hotel's visitors, and fools the clerk into revealing information about them.

As they are walking upstairs, they run into Sir Henry, who is angry because another of his boots is missing. He has no explanation for the disappearance.

Later, after lunch in the hotel room, Holmes approves of Sir Henry's decision to inhabit Baskerville Hall, since it will allow Holmes to flush out the culprit more easily than he can in crowded London. From Dr. Mortimer, Holmes and Watson learn that the only moor resident with a black beard is Barrymore, Baskerville Hall's butler. Intrigued, Holmes orders a telegram sent to Devonshire, to determine whether Barrymore is there.

Mortimer then discusses the contents of Sir Charles's will, in the hopes of sussing out a murder motive. Barrymore and his wife inherited money from Sir Charles's will, and they were aware of that intention. However, Dr. Mortimer adds that several people - himself included - were bequeathed money by the will. Sir Henry was naturally left the most money, and because he has no direct heir, that fortune and the estate would fall to some distant cousins, the Desmonds, if were to die.

Holmes then proposes that Watson accompany Sir Henry to Baskerville Hall, as protection. Holmes will join them that Saturday, after completing some business on another case in London.

Before the men leave, Sir Henry finds one of his brown boot under a cabinet, which is confusing since Mortimer had thoroughly searched the room before lunch. They surmise a waiter had found and placed it there, but the waiter knows nothing of it when he is called and questioned.

That evening, Watson and Holmes receive two telegrams. The first is a return telegram from Barrymore, suggesting that he is indeed at Baskerville Hall. The second reports that Cartwright has been unable to find the cut sheet of the newspaper.

At that moment, the cab driver, whom Holmes had sent for earlier, appears at the door. He tells Holmes that the bearded man had claimed to be a detective, and had told him to say nothing to anyone. Strangest of all, the man had claimed to be named

"Mr. Sherlock Holmes" (188). Holmes is surprised and amused.

He pays the cab driver for details of the day's journey, and then sends the driver away. Noting that "our third thread" has snapped, Holmes admires his adversary as "worthy of our steel" (189). He then wishes Watson luck in Devonshire, noting that this case is proving to be an ugly business.

Analysis

In this section, three "threads" lead to dead-ends. On the one hand, this presents obstacles that challenge our detective. However, it is crucial to realize that even dead-ends provide central questions and clues for one as perceptive as Holmes. For instance: Who would steal a boot, then return it? How did this person get into the hotel unbeknownst to Holmes, Watson, Dr. Mortimer, and Sir Henry? Who could be so clever as to pose as Holmes? Does the mystery man in the cab already know who Sherlock Holmes is?

The criminal here proves to be as cunning as the detective, as Holmes himself declares that he has been "checkmated" (189). In other words, the wits of the detective and criminal are matched here. This is important for two reasons. The first is that it keeps the story interesting; the story gains momentum only because the adversary can think like the hero, and hence complicate the latter's pursuit of his objective. However, it is also important in context, considering that this was one of the later Holmes novels. Audiences would have been familiar with Holmes's genius by this point, and hence would themselves grow bored if the mystery were not beyond even the hero.

And yet the criminal's genius is important for Holmes as well. Notice his response to having been fooled; he laughs. It is a central part of Holmes's character - one that later writers have capitalized on even more than Doyle did - that Holmes is motivated by the game, and not by empathy. In other words, he does not want to solve the case to help someone - if he did, an easy victory would be preferable. Instead, he wants to be tested so that he can triumph. The criminal's trickery complicates his mission, and hence makes his eventual victory all the more satisfying.

Another character insight is provided by the museum visit at the top of this chapter. Though only a short paragraph, the incident touches on the elusive nature of genius. Holmes is able to divert his attention when there is no path to follow, again suggesting that he is not at all affected by the human element of his story. He is not worried about people, but only about the case. When the case is momentarily cold, he chooses to spend his time elsewhere. However, the idea that he would study paintings also provides some insight into Doyle's depiction of the mind, which employs both subconscious and conscious faculties to reach its potential. Certainly, there are times when Holmes confronts a problem through deliberate thought, but there are then others when he does not think explicitly on the case, leaving his mind to work in the background while he focuses on something else.

Some insight is given into the nature of Watson and Holmes's relationship in this chapter as well. Watson is surprised to hear that Holmes has volunteered him to accompany Sir Henry. What is implied here - and in the first chapter, when Holmes has Watson attempt to interpret Dr. Mortimer's walking stick - is a level of condescension that Holmes employs towards his friend. Watson is so immediately pleased to be of use that we are led to realize that he is not frequently of much use, at least not in a way that Holmes acknowledges. This inconsideration is made more explicit later, when Watson finds that Holmes is merely using him as a pawn in his greater game.

Summary and Analysis of Chapter VI

Summary

Chapter VI: Baskerville Hall

On the day of Watson, Dr. Mortimer and Sir Henry's departure, Holmes drives Watson to the station. En route, he instructs Watson to report only the facts to him, leaving his theories out of the letters. He also shares his own theories. He does not believes that the Desmond man - who would inherit Sir Henry's estate - is involved, but he believes that Barrymore and his wife are viable suspects. His other suspects include: a groom at the Hall, two farmers on the moor, Dr. Mortimer himself, Mortimer's wife, Stapleton the naturalist, and Mr. Frankland. (These names were provided by Mortimer in their early discussions.) Watson has brought his gun, in case he needs it.

When they arrive in Devonshire, Sir Henry is impressed by the surroundings, never having seen the moor before. Watson imagines what it must be like for him to see the land where the men of his blood have made their mark.

On their way to Baskerville Hall, they meet a man guarding part of the moor. Apparently, a convict had escaped three days earlier from the prison at nearby Princetown. This convict's name is Selden, and he is known as the Notting Hill murderer. Watson recalls Sherlock's interest in that case because of the criminal's brutality, and imagines Selden hiding out on the moor.

At Baskerville Hall, Dr. Mortimer shows Sir Henry the yew alley where Sir Charles died, and then departs. Barrymore then tours them around the estate, admitting in the process that he and his wife plan to leave once Sir Henry has hired more staff. Having spent their lives there, they would like to travel with the money Sir Charles bequeathed them.

Watson describes the bedrooms as seeming newer the rest of the house, and the dining room as having a somber atmosphere. Feeling the same way, Sir Henry comments that he understands why Sir Charles grew so anxious in such a place.

That night, Watson does not sleep well. In the dead of night, he hears a woman's sob, and listens carefully for more. However, no more noise comes.

Analysis

The chapter begins with Holmes's instructions to Watson to "report the facts" (191). Most immediately, Holmes's instructions touch on why he trusts Watson as a good "conductor of light" (138). Watson inspires Holmes's genius not by collaborating on his interpretations, but rather on relating facts that Holmes can then use to deduce hidden truths. As a doctor, Watson is well-acquainted with the importance of detail, an approach Holmes takes to a singular level.

However, these instructions also pose a crucial question: what does a bare fact look like? Can we describe facts without already having some explanation as to how that fact came to be? Put another way, can a fact ever be disclosed without containing some trace of interpretation? For example, in Chapter II, Sir Charles's footprints of Sir Charles are described as "tiptoe" footprints (164). The description contained within it an assumption. Whereas most readers would take this interpretation as fact, Holmes took a step back to consider that the indentations might indicate the opposite: running instead of tip-toeing. By describing something, we naturally put an interpretation on it. In other words, so-called "facts" already come pre-interpreted (191).

Holmes's instructions then, are most notable for what he instructs Watson *not* to do: to theorize. What makes Holmes's approach so unique is that he considers a detail from several possible angles at once, eliminating impossible options to determine the most likely option. His instructions are not only to Watson, but to us: to correctly deduce meaning, one must first see the detail in itself, not with any pre-conceived notion.

Watson's description of the house both conforms to and works against those instructions. He makes judgments - the rooms seems newer than the rest of the house - and in fact focuses on atmosphere. His failure to simply 'describe' the rooms are entirely forgivable, especially since they help to relate the atmosphere that would have made Sir Charles so anxious.

Watson's description also serve Doyle's purpose of crafting an engaging and spooky tale. One of the novel's most intriguing contrasts - between the supernatural and the rational - is at work here. Clearly, Doyle wants us to view this location as haunted and possessed. The moor was often used as an atmospheric locale in the work of British writers, and Doyle takes great advantage of its natural allure. In fact, he furthers the atmosphere through the incident of the woman's screams. Read out of context, the second half of this chapter could work in a Gothic novel, or even in a children's scary story.

The contrast with the rational will be most clearly made through Holmes's interference, but is already present through Sir Henry. His first instinct at noting the house's gloominess is to brighten it with electric lamps. He represents the technological mindset of America, from which he has traveled. He is more like Holmes than he is like Dr. Mortimer; instead of considering the house's haunted potential, he considers how the products of man's rationality might counteract such gloominess. Whether he will remain so aloof to its spooky atmosphere now becomes one of the novel's dramatic questions.

Summary and Analysis of Chapter VII-IX

Summary

Chapter VII: The Stapletons of Merripit House

The house seems more cheerful in the fresh light of the next day, so Sir Henry speculates that the gloom was merely in their imaginations. When Watson mentions the woman's cry, Sir Henry recalls the sound but had dismissed it as a dream. They question Barrymore to learn that there are only two women in the house; he is certain that Mrs. Barrymore was not the screamer. However, when Watson meets Mrs. Barrymore, he notices signs that she had been crying the night before, and assumes that Mr. Barrymore has lied to them.

Watson therefore decides to investigate whether Barrymore was actually at Baskerville, as his telegram had indicated. He visits the postmaster at nearby Grimpen, who had insisted that he placed the initial telegram directly into Barrymore's hands. Upon interrogation, however, he admits that he actually delivered the telegram to Mrs. Barrymore, who promised to pass it along to her husband. Assuming Barrymore was the bearded man, Watson's only theory is that Barrymore was attempting to scare Sir Henry away from London so that he and Mrs. Barrymore could have the manor to themselves, but he admits that theory is inadequate.

As Watson is walking back to Baskerville, Stapleton "the naturalist" overtakes him (163). Having learned about Watson from Dr. Mortimer, Stapleton shares his own theory about Sir Charles's death: the man's anxieties had grown so great that the appearance of a random dog led to his death. Stapleton also surprises Watson by asking about Holmes's opinions on the matter; he insists that the detective is well-known even on the moor.

Watson hesitates when Stapleton invites him home (to Merripit House) to meet his sister Miss Stapleton, but then decides to go. As they walk there, Stapleton indicates the Grimpen Mire, a place where men or animals can disappear into the quicksand-like ground if they are not careful. Bragging that he has discovered the two safe paths through the mire, Stapleton describes the peaceful natural scenery on the other side. When Watson professes an interest in seeing it, Stapleton insists that one should not brave the danger without knowing the landmarks as he does.

Suddenly, Watson hears a dull murmur which swells into a deep roar. Though Stapleton admits that locals believe this is the sound of the dreaded hound, he dismisses such conjecture, claiming the sound must have a perfectly natural cause.

When they arrive near Merripit House, Watson sees Miss Stapleton outside, and notices that she is beautiful, almost the opposite of her brother. Immediately,

Stapleton spies an insect and rushes to collect it. Away from her brother's notice, before even introducing herself, Miss Stapleton commands Watson to return to London. He barely has time to question her before Stapleton returns and introduces them formally, at which point she is surprised to learn he is not Sir Henry, as she had thought.

They walk towards the house, and Stapleton reveals that he had once managed a school, but lost it when an epidemic took the lives of three students. He had lost most of his money in the venture, and Miss Stapleton is now unhappy to live so far away from civilization.

After asking for permission to visit Sir Henry, Stapleton invites Watson to view his insect collection. However, Watson insists he should return, and sets off for Baskerville Hall. He is not far from Merripit when Miss Stapleton intercepts him and asks him to ignore her warning. Watson offers to convey the warning to Sir Henry if she will explain it, but she offers nothing other than a reiteration of her fear. She also asks him to keep this secret from her brother, since he believes it necessary that someone live in Baskerville Hall, since the moor locals rely on the Baskerville philanthropy.

Chapter VIII: First Report of Dr. Watson

This is the first of two chapters that are comprised of Watson's letters to Holmes. He notes, however, that one page is missing from the letter.

This first letter is dated October 13th, written from Baskerville Hall. Watson begins by describing the effects the moor has on the soul: he feels about though he is amongst prehistoric man, rather than in modern England.

Watson explains that the locals believe Selden has left the area, since it has been two weeks since his escape. He also confesses his worry for the Stapletons, who live far removed from their closest neighbor. He then notes that Sir Henry seems to be romantically interested in Beryl Stapleton. However, he worries that Stapleton himself - who had recently shown Watson the place of Hugo Baskerville's fabled death - would not approve of a match between them.

Watson then describes his interactions with others. Dr. Mortimer had recently toured him through the yew alley where Sir Charles died. Meanwhile, Watson has visited Mr. Frankland, of Lafter Hall, whom Watson explains is well known and frequently distrusted for his litigious nature. He is slowly spending his fortune on lawsuits, many of which are arbitrary and rooted in outdated laws. Frankland is also an amateur astronomer; he owns a telescope.

In the last section of the letter, Watson describes what he considers the most essential element of his visit thus far: the continuing mystery of the Barrymores. Sir Henry asked Barrymore directly whether he had received the telegram, and the man, surprised, confirmed that Mrs. Barrymore had given it to him. Watson continues to note the signs of crying on Mrs. Barrymore, and worries that her husband is abusive. The night before writing this letter, Watson had awoken at 2:00 a.m. and saw a man who looked like Barrymore crossing the moor towards the house, and then entering an unoccupied part of the house. Watson snuck after him, and saw the man peering out of the window. After a while, Barrymore groaned and then left for his room. Later that night, Watson heard a key turn in a lock.

Chapter IX: The Second Report of Dr. Watson: The Light upon the Moor

This letter is dated October 15th.

Two days after seeing Barrymore in the room, Watson examined it to find it has "the nearest outlook on the moor" (225). Hence, he believes Mr. Barrymore was looking for something on the moor. Initially, he believed the man was meeting a lover, but then disregarded that notion as unfounded.

Sir Henry was not surprised to hear Watson's report on that night's events, and they decided to follow the man out onto the moor one night. After agreeing on the plan, Sir Henry prepared to set out, and refused Watson permission to accompany him as protection. Watson followed him anyway, to find he was meeting Miss Stapleton.

From afar, Watson observed them in a heated argument. When Sir Henry attempted to kiss her, Stapleton himself suddenly appeared and entered the argument. After the Stapletons departed, Watson approached Sir Henry, and apologized for snooping, explaining that he was only keeping his promise to Holmes. Though initially annoyed, Sir Henry laughed off the transgression, and then confessed his belief that Stapleton was crazy. This had been his first time alone with Miss Stapleton, who was begging him to leave the moor. When Sir Henry promised to leave if she would accompany him, Stapleton had interrupted them. The man is confused why the brother would so strongly oppose such an advantageous match for his sister. Watson is equally confused by the behavior.

Later that afternoon, Stapleton visited Baskerville Hall to apologize. He promised to approve the match if Sir Henry will wait three months before proposing.

Watson then changes the topic to another "thread" of the mystery (233). One night, he and Sir Henry followed Barrymore to the room. Sir Henry confronted the butler, who initially claimed he was only fastening the window. When pressed, the butler then admitted he was holding a candle to the window for someone's benefit, but refused to reveal any more. Watson then noticed another candle light across the moor. When Sir Henry threatened to fire the man, Mrs. Barrymore appeared and admitted the truth: the convict Selden is her brother, and they were leaving food nightly for him. She explained that he had always been spoiled as a child, and that she feels responsible for him.

Sir Henry withdraws his threat to Barrymore, and then he and Watson set out to capture Selden. It begins to rain as they are out on the moor, and they then hear that strange cry Watson had heard earlier. Sir Henry was visibly frightened, especially when Watson admitted that locals believed this to be the cry of the Hound of the Baskervilles.

When the men reached the light across the moor, they initially found no one there. Watson suddenly spotted the criminal fleeing, and they set out in pursuit. However, Selden hurled a large rock and them, and then outran them.

In the distance, Watson noticed a figure silhouetted by the lightning. He indicated the figure to Sir Henry, but it disappeared before the latter saw it. Sir Henry speculated that this was a guard looking for the convict, but Watson was clearly not entirely convinced.

Analysis

In these chapters, Sir Henry and Watson begin to fall prey to superstition because of the gloomy atmosphere of both the house and the moor. They are no longer protected by bustling, urban life, which tends to support a more rational outlook. One reason that superstition is less associated with urban life is the plethora of witnesses: there are always many people who see an event, and hence is there less room for occult mythology to grow. In the country, there is a lot more space, and there are fewer people who witness events. When they do see these events, they see them from far away. All of this makes it easier for legends like that of the hound to perpetuate. For instance, the sound that Watson hears is easily attributed to the mythical hound since it is occurring far away from any witness who can testify to its true cause. The moor symbolizes the seemingly occult and mysterious ways of nature, which may seem not always act according to explainable, natural law. Several factors - the townspeople whom Watson sees as primitive, the figure in the distance, and of course the sound of the hound - all feed this strange atmosphere.

Associated with this theme of the supernatural is the theme of evil. Evil seems to pervade the moor, and the legend of Henry Baskerville paints the picture of an unequivocally evil man, almost more a metaphor than a human. Similarly, Selden is a figure known to be vicious and dangerous. The unknown figure in the distance carries just as much potential for evil, considering the rainy atmosphere in which he is first scene, and that ever-present threat of the hound. All of these figures are most frightening because Watson knows nothing about them. Like Henry Baskerville does, they seem to represent a darkness, an evil.

However, evil is itself an expression of superstition and irrationalism. Therefore, the stakes for Watson - who is attempting to combat his growing superstition with his intellectual will - are larger than simply remaining untouched with country legends. He also must resist the temptation to see the world in terms of moral evil, rather than in terms of human psychology and motive, the realm that Holmes operates in.

This conflict - between inherent evil and nuanced rationality - is also explored through Doyle's attitude towards criminality. It is notable that Dr. Watson describes Selden as a "crafty and savage animal," and mentions that he has an "evil yellow face" (241). This description is symptomatic of a larger belief in the unchangeable and savage nature of the criminal, popular during that time period. Even Mrs. Barrymore does not seem to believe that her brother is able to be reformed into a civilized person. However, she does explain the circumstances by which he became a criminal. Thus, Doyle is attempting to comment on such strict beliefs, offering a more modernized attitude to criminality, as caused less by inherent evil than by circumstance. Though the novel does not explicitly address questions of reform, it does apply Holmes's more nuanced understanding - that generalized types are only the first step towards understand individuals - to a pressing social question.

The difficulty of observing pure facts continues to resonate in these chapters. For instance, Watson does not notice much about Stapleton, and attempts to refrain from noting the man's strangeness (since that would constitute an impression rather than a fact). However, it is somewhat clear to the reader that Stapleton is a suspicious character. His over-eagerness, his almost arrogantly delivered knowledge of the moor and of Holmes's celebrity, and his fixation on his sister are all signs of his strangeness. It is unclear whether Watson misses these signs, or simply does not want to taint his reports to Holmes with subjective impressions, but the way he relates the man to the reader offers us some clues.

On a side note, Stapleton's professed knowledge - of the moors and of Holmes - conforms the novel's greater theme of knowledge as power. Because of what he knows, he is able to control others and shape impressions. In the same way that Holmes uses information as a key, Stapleton uses knowledge as a tool, in ways that become clearer as the story progresses.

It is notable that Chapters VIII and IX are related as letters. There is an earlier novelistic form known as the epistolary novel, a story told entirely through letters sent between characters. Doyle is not simply staging an homage to this tradition, however. Instead, the use of the letters - and later of Watson's diaries - conform to the greater themes of observation and subjectivity. Whereas most of the novel is framed as Watson's story told from hindsight to readers, these letters are written at the time of the event, to Holmes himself. Therefore, they reflect his viewpoint, his attempt to make sense of the facts he observes. Later, we realize how inadequate his interpretations are, but Doyle's intent is not to mock Watson, but rather to illustrate how the art of deduction begins with the art of proper observation. Finally, the use of these varied formats adds an air of verisimilitude to the story, helping it feel true and accurate, obviously an important effect for a story so concerned with themes of rationality.

Also, Watson's voyeuristic nature is made explicit in the letters. We tend to associate Watson with the impartial observer: he is not the active hero of the story, but rather the third party. What this also means is that we know very little of Watson's private life. Earlier, Holmes noted that Watson spends so much time at his club because he lacks many personal friends. This character approach reveals a distinction between the detective story and other, more traditional novels. These more traditional novels tend to give us privileged access to private spaces: the minds of others, bedrooms, and other interior, private spaces. In other words, most novels and stories are primarily concerned with the psychology of their heroes. Watson, on the other hand, serves a plot function in many ways. Though he does attempt to self-correct his snooping observations of Sir Henry, apologizing for his behavior, he is clearly a man driven to watch from a hidden vantage, as evidenced on the night that he trails Barrymore. If he was not this kind of person, then the story's progress would be significantly hampered.

Finally, the reader at this point may wonder why Holmes has not yet appeared to investigate the crime scene. These chapters mostly feature Dr. Watson in action. Though he is able to disentangle one thread of the mystery, he is clearly making slow progress. Further, he shows independence, disobeying Holmes's instructions by allowing Sir Henry to head out onto the moor at night. And yet he is well aware that his progress is limited, confessing in Chapter IX that they need Holmes. Clearly, Doyle is well aware of what his readers would want at this point, and moves quickly to remedy his hero's absence.

Summary and Analysis of Chapter X-XI

Summary

Chapter X: Extract from the Diary of Dr. Watson

This chapter is taken directly from Watson's diary, which he insists is the best way to tell this part of the story.

The first entry is dated October 16th, the day after Watson and Sir Henry pursued Selden on the moor. Owing to the ominous mood of his surroundings and the frightening sounds he had twice heard, Watson almost believed in the hound. Though the diary acknowledges that such a belief strains his rationality, he also admits the "facts" of the howling, and acknowledge the difficulties posed even if there were an actual hound (245). For instance, the hound would need to be fed.

Watson then considers the mystery of the bearded man in London, noting that he has seen no one resembling that figure out on the moor. He decided to concentrate on this problem, hoping it would open doors to some of the other mysteries.

That morning, Barrymore was upset that Watson and Sir Henry had attempted to capture Selden. He promised them that the convict would soon escape to South America, and cause no more trouble for them. They then agreed not to pursue Selden any further.

Grateful, Barrymore then revealed a secret about Sir Charles: he was planning to meet a woman in the yew alley on the night that he died. However, Barrymore knows only the woman's initials - L.L. - and that she had sent Sir Charles a letter from Coombe Tracey, the nearby town, on the day of his death. Mrs. Barrymore had found the remnants of this letter, half-burned in Sir Charles's study. Barrymore explained that he concealed this information for fear it would damage his master's reputation.

Watson then immediately wrote to Holmes with this new information, hoping that his friend would soon complete his other work in London and join them on the moor.

The next diary entry is dated the next day, October 17th. Watson traveled back to the spot from which he had seen the mysterious figure, but found nothing.

On his way back, Dr. Mortimer intercepted him. The man was driving a dog-cart and looking for his missing spaniel. Watson mentioned the initials L.L. to the doctor, who recognized them as belonging to Laura Lyons, the daughter of Frankland. She had married an artist who deserted her, and her father had practically disowned her. She now lived in Coombe Tracey. Though grateful, Watson did not explain the relevance of the initials.

Later that day, Barrymore told Watson that Selden had seemingly left the moor, and that the convict had also seen the mysterious figure. Selden believed the figure to be that of a gentleman who received his food from Coombe Tracey, and knew that the man was living in one of the old deserted houses on the moor.

Chapter XI: The Man on the Tor

This chapter returns to Watson's direct narration.

Watson and Sir Henry discuss the new information about Laura Lyons, and decide Watson should visit her alone, in hopes of obtaining more information that way.

In his visit, Watson notices her beauty right away. He first introduces himself as a friend of Frankland, but she quickly dismisses any interest in the man. Watson then admits he is inquiring about Sir Charles, and hoping to avoid a public scandal. Growing nervous then angry, she initially denies asking him to meet her but backtracks when Watson quotes the portion of the letter that Mrs. Barrymore had found. She swears that she never kept her appointment because of another circumstance she does not wish to discuss. When Watson threatens to involve the police, she confesses the contents of the letter: her husband was pressuring her to move back with him, and she was borrowing money from Sir Charles to ensure her freedom. She did not keep the appointment because she received the money from somewhere else.

Believing her story plausible, Watson resolves to investigate whether she had actually filed divorce proceedings. However, he remains troubled by her manner in telling the story: she had turned pale, and had to be coaxed into admitting most of the details.

Watson's next plan is to hunt for the mysterious figure he had seen on the Black Tor, believing this might be the bearded man from London. However, he does not know how to begin, since there are many old houses and transient residents out on the moor.

Good luck comes when he visits Old Frankland, who tells Watson about the several legal cases he is involved in. Watson pretends to be indifferent, knowing that any outward sign of interest will silence Frankland's gossip. Frankland eventually discusses the figure, believing it to be of the convict. Through his telescope, he has seen a child leaving food for the man. Watson uses the telescope to pinpoint the spot, and then swears he will keep Frankland's secret.

Watson then travels to the stone huts in that area, and recognizes signs of habitation near one of them. He carefully sneaks in, but finds only a sheet of paper in the hut, announcing his own visit to Coombe Tracey. Watson immediately realizes that he is the object of pursuit, rather than Sir Henry. With his gun ready, he resolves to wait for the man's return.

When he hears the man arrive, he cocks his pistol. However, the figure who enters the hut is none other than Sherlock Holmes himself.

Analysis

The section begins with Watson's own doubts: he wants to believe himself a man of pure reason, but the facts simply do not suggest a rational explanation. He therefore considers the possibility of a supernatural hound, even though that offends his rationality. Watson's process here is one that Holmes (and Doyle) would likely applaud: the attempt to pursue a rational explanation even when our instincts drive us towards occult explanations. Deep down, we should continue to pursue scientific explanations, even when one is not immediately apparent. Ultimately, this process is what draws Holmes towards difficult cases rather than simple ones.

In attempting this process, Watson - rather than Holmes - becomes our detective. His process is quite commendable: instead of trying to solve the entire mystery at once, he focuses on a single thread, hoping that it might yield clues to keep the investigation alive. In trying to determine who the mystery man is, Watson ends up following a wandering path that does yield several clues, including: the details of L.L. and some evidence about the mysterious figure. What this process indicates is that an explanation of one aspect of reality may surprisingly help explain another. The implicit suggestion is that we turn to occult explanations because we are overwhelmed by too many questions at once, whereas we might discover more scientific rationales if we attempt to answer one question at a time.

During this investigation, Watson feels as though he is caught in a large "net" (267). This image is a symbol of the power yielded by those who have knowledge. This is a common theme throughout the novel: knowledge brings power. The detective almost necessarily starts behind the criminal (who has already perpetuated, planned and executed a crime before the detective is brought in). Hence, the chase is about gaining knowledge so as to limit the criminal of his singular power. This is another reason why one should pursue one detail at a time, rather than attempt to solve the mystery in one fell swoop. While the latter process obscures crucial clues, the former involves a process of collecting knowledge one step at a time.

Note an interesting bit of phrasing that develops this metaphor of the next. When Watson is approaching the huts where he believes the mysterious figure lives, he "walk[s] as warily as Stapleton would do when with poised net he drew near the settled butterfly" (266). The net here implies in the basic sense that Watson is approaching knowledge. However, it also foreshadows the fact that Stapleton is the one controlling the net, the one who knows more than anyone else. Because of this knowledge, he is manipulating events even as Watson and Holmes close the gap. Again, even with the villain, the novel suggests that man's ultimate power comes not from his strength but from his mind.

And of course, Watson gains a rather startling bit of information because of his investigation: the mystery figure is actually Sherlock Holmes himself! As the detective will explain in the following chapters, there is a perfectly logical reason for his subterfuge, but it raises a variety of questions that the reader himself can enjoy considering. Holmes is ahead of both Watson and us as readers, which poses us with the challenge of filling in the gaps.

Summary and Analysis of Chapter XII-XIII

Summary

Chapter XII: Death on the Moor

Watson is naturally astounded, and more than a little offended, to find Holmes there. Having been kept out of the loop, he believes his reports have been wasted, and that Holmes has used him as a pawn. However, Holmes insists that Watson's reports - which were stopped at Combe Tracey and brought to Holmes by Cartwright, whom accompanied Holmes from London - have proven extremely useful. Holmes deduces how Watson found him and then asks for what new information he learned in his visit to Laura Lyons.

After Watson shares his information, Holmes shares his own: there is record of a relationship between Stapleton and Laura, leading Holmes to believe Stapleton the culprit. Holmes has uncovered that Miss Stapleton is actually Stapleton's wife, not his sister. This is why Stapleton so vehemently opposed any union between her and Sir Henry. Through research, Holmes has learned that Stapleton was indeed a schoolmaster who lost his job, but that he had operated under a different name and then disappeared without a trace. Holmes has deduced that not only was Stapleton the bearded man in London, but that his wife must have been the person who tried to warn them. Clearly, Stapleton believes he can gain some benefit from lying about his wife's identity.

Right as Holmes admits that Stapleton's plan must be murder, the men hear the hound's cries out on the moor. They rush out towards the direction of the sound, Holmes lamenting that Stapleton has struck before Holmes could ensnare him. As they arrive near the source of the sound, they hear a human moan and then see a body fall from a great height. They recognize Sir Henry's clothes on the figure, and realize their charge is dead.

They both blame themselves - Watson for leaving Sir Henry alone, Holmes for having delayed his action - and then climb onto the rocks to try and spot the hound. Instead, they spot the Stapleton house and briefly plan how to ensnare the culprit. Suddenly, Holmes realizes that the corpse has a beard - it is not Sir Henry, but Selden! Watson realizes that Barrymore must have given Sir Henry's extra clothes to the man.

They then wonder two things: why Selden would have been so frightened of the sound, and why Stapleton would have thought to release the hound on this night.

Before they can answer either, Selden strolls up, surprised to see them. His surprise is even greater, though, to discover the convict's body. He claims he heard the sound as well, and then quickly identifies Holmes. The men talk vaguely as Holmes sizes him up, and then decide they must leave the body with something over its face until the next day.

Chapter XIII: Fixing the Nets

As they walk across the moor, Holmes explains to Watson that they lack sufficient evidence to secure Stapleton's arrest. They have neither determined a motive nor actually seen the hound. Holmes plans to tell Laura Lyons about Stapleton's marriage, in hopes that she will then work with them against him.

Before they arrive at Baskerville Hall, Holmes warns Watson not to say anything of the hound. Pleased to see Holmes has arrived, Sir Henry joins the men at dinner. Before they eat, Watson breaks the news of Selden to Barrymore and his wife, who are quite saddened.

As they dine, Sir Henry tells them that Stapleton had invited him to dinner that night, but that he did not want to break his promise to stay away from the moor at night.

Holmes then drily remarks that the convict had been wearing Sir Henry's clothes when he died. In response to Sir Henry's surprise, Holmes begins to lay out a plan, but his attention is struck by the line of portraits on the opposite wall. He observes that Hugo Baskerville looks quite meek in his portrait, and Sir Henry adds that the canvas is dated 1647.

After dinner, Holmes brings Watson to the portrait and leads the latter to recognize that the picture resembles Stapleton, if one ignores the hair and focuses solely on the facial shape. They have finally discovered the missing link of their mystery: Stapleton is a Baskerville!

The next morning, Holmes instructs Sir Henry to dine that night with the Stapletons, and to travel there alone. He further tells him that he and Watson intend to return to London, on urgent business. Though upset at being abandoned, Sir Henry agrees to follow Holmes's instructions.

Watson and Holmes head to the train station, to perpetuate the ruse. There, Holmes directs Cartwright to take the train and to send a telegram from London to Sir Henry Baskerville. Cartwright also delivers a telegram that had arrived for Holmes, from Inspector Lestrade, a London police officer. The message informs Holmes that Lestrade will arrive later that day with an unsigned warrant.

Watson and Holmes then visit Laura Lyons. Holmes is very straightforward with her: he accuses her of withholding information that pertains to Sir Charles's death, and informs her that he believes she is implicated alongside Stapleton and his wife for it. Though shocked, she is eventually convinced that the man is indeed married. She then cooperates, explaining that Stapleton had offered to marry her if she could get divorced, but then had convinced her to break her appointment with Sir Charles, promising he could obtain the money himself. Finally, he had frightened her into remaining silent, suggesting she would be found guilty for his death. Holmes tells her she is lucky to remain alive.

After they leave, Holmes declares that they will be able to construct a cohesive narrative of the mystery by the end of that night. They then fetch Lestrade from the train station and head into Dartmoor, where Baskerville Manor is located.

Analysis

Holmes' investigation finally begins to yield results, as the metaphoric 'net' is transferred into his court. Significantly, we discover that his game of detection is a game of wits: Holmes must figure out how to trick Stapleton into believing he is really uninterested in the case. First, this approach parallels Stapleton's own. Both men lead others to assume things about them, rather than forcing those impressions on others.

Further, both men have certain personal habits in common. Consider the esoteric behavior attributed to Homes in the early chapters. His daily life and habits are quite disorderly, and he lacks a certain social intelligence. The meticulousness of his method is at great odds with his daily habits. This suggests Doyle's belief that a life purely of the mind has little room for the trappings of a 'normal' life.

Secondly, this game of wits is complicated by the necessity of proving his deductions before the law. Though in many ways a pawn in the plot, Lestrade is also a crucial component; if he does not witness the crime, then Holmes's brilliance can yield no dividends. His own interpretation cannot reach the level of truth until it can create conviction in two senses: readerly conviction and legal conviction. Holmes must endanger characters in the novel because his interpretation may not otherwise fulfill both of these requirements. When he laments the death of Sir Henry (who is actually Selden, of course) he is lamenting this shortcoming, the fact that he had to risk the man's life in order to secure both convictions of the culprit.

In other words, this necessity for legal status parallels Doyle's requirements to make this story an "interesting" case (192). It is notable that the detective story usually consists of a crime that is committed in the past, and investigated in the present. However, the investigation might sometime seems dull if it did not itself involve crime and action. Here then we have that crime coming alive. History is here repeating itself.

The conflict between Holmes and Watson reaches its apex in Chapter XII, when Watson accuses Holmes of using him. Later, Holmes calls Watson a man of "action," contrasting that with his own intellectual nature. In many ways, Holmes *does* use Watson as he uses anyone else. Knowing his friend's active nature, he had to keep Watson in the dark in order to best use that personality trait. That Holmes cannot empathize with Watson's sense of betrayal is just one of the sacrifices he makes to follow his own singular path. Action is important, but must always be subsumed to the intellect, which alone holds the power. For Doyle and Holmes, this is true both in ourselves and in the symbolic representation of Holmes and Watson.

Finally, it is notable that women are not presented in a very flattering way in this novel. Holmes never really had love interests, and the novel's only deep relationship is the friendship between Holmes and Watson. Here, despite her good intentions, Miss Stapleton is used mostly as a foil, to both the villain and Sir Henry. Laura Lyons, moreover, is motivated solely by finding the proper husband, and is easily manipulated by Stapleton and then by Holmes. Overall, women tend not to be as clever as men in Doyle's work, and they are often too fearful for their own lives to be of much help. Clearly, gender was not a primary theme in Doyle's mind, but his representation of women leaves much to be desired for a modern reader.

Summary and Analysis of Chapter XIV-XV

Summary

Chapter XIV: The Hound of the Baskervilles

The men - Watson, Holmes, and Lestrade - take up position about 200 yards from Merripit House, each armed with a pistol. Filled with anticipation, Watson sneaks closer to the house, and sees Sir Henry and Stapleton drinking inside. Miss Stapleton is nowhere to be seen. After a few minutes, Stapleton leaves the house and enters a nearby out-house. While he is inside, Watson hears some sounds from within. After Stapleton returns to the main house, Watson reports back to the others.

Meanwhile, a fog begins to roll in, upsetting Holmes since it will compromise their visibility. They retreat a bit, to find some higher ground. From that vantage, they soon see Sir Henry anxiously pass. A moment later, Holmes cries out that the hound is coming. As quickly as he registers Holmes's terror, Watson sees an enormous hound, which does not look mortal at all. Fire bursts from its mouth and its body sparkles in the night. All three men are paralyzed by the savage sight.

Regaining their composure, Holmes and Watson shoot at the beast. Though the shots do not stop it, it does cry out in pain. Holmes chases after the beast, and finds it prepared to tear out Sir Henry's throat. Holmes shoots the animal five times, killing it.

Sir Henry is unwounded, but paralyzed in fear. They examine the hound's corpse, to discover that it is cross-breed of mastiff and bloodhound. Phosphorus has been placed around its muzzle, which explains why it seemed to spew fire, and its fur was covered with a glittery substance.

Holmes then leads the others towards Stapleton, whom he fears has fled after hearing gunshots. The culprit's house is empty, though they find there that Miss Stapleton has been tied up and gagged in a locked room full of collected butterflies and moths. Her first inquiry after being released is for Sir Henry. Crying, she claims she would have suffered Stapleton's abuse had he actually loved her, but she now knows she was only his pawn. She also tells them that he probably fled to an old tin mine on an island in the heart of Grimpen Mire. This was the place where he kept the hound locked away.

They decide not to pursue Stapleton that night, since there are too many dangerous pitfalls in Grimpen Mire. Miss Stapleton adds that even Stapleton himself will have faced dangers attempting the perilous path at night.

The next morning, Sir Henry falls into a delirious fever. Watson tells the reader that the man does not recover until after a year of world travels, taken with Dr. Mortimer as companion.

Miss Stapleton leads Holmes and Watson out into the mire, where they find nothing but Stapleton's boot, and therefore assume that he was lost in the bog while trying to escape. They also find traces of Mortimer's dog, as well as gnawed bones which suggest that Stapleton fed the hound in this place. Lastly, Holmes finds some paste in a tin, which he believes holds a trace of the phosphorus used.

The main story ends as Holmes admits that Stapleton is the most dangerous man he has ever tracked.

Chapter XV: A Retrospection

In this final chapter, Watson recounts everything Holmes later told him about the case.

At the end of November, about a month after the events near Baskerville, Watson feels comfortable asking for more information, since Holmes has since solved two other cases. Holmes declares that the case was only difficult because they did not know Stapleton's motive, but that he has learned much from two long conversations with Miss Stapleton.

Stapleton - as Holmes continues to call him - was the son of Rodger Baskerville, Sir Charles's younger brother. When he died in South America, Rodger left behind one son, also named Rodger. This boy, who would later be known as Stapleton, stole money and fled to England, where he set up a school and changed his name to Vandeleur. When the school failed, he made inquiries into the Baskerville estate, and then moved to Devonshire. Though he had not yet formed an exact plan, he cultivated a friendship with Sir Charles and passed Beryl off as his sister. It was there that he learned about the legend of the hound, as well as about Sir Charles's weak heart and innate fear of the legend. It was then that he concocted his plan: he bought a large dog in London, devised the artificial means of making the creature seem so fearsome, and intended to use his wife to lure Sir Charles out into the moor at night. However, when she refused, he struck up a relationship with Laura Lyons to accomplish that purpose.

Laura lured Sir Charles out that night by appealing to his mercy; he was going to give her money to secure her divorce. Stapleton convinced her not to go, and set the hound out, which terrified poor Sir Charles to death. The hound then retreated, leaving the pawprint that Dr. Mortimer would later see. Both women at that point suspected Stapleton of the murder, but were too much under his influence to take any action.

When Sir Henry was set to arrive to England, Stapleton took his wife with him to London, as he distrusted her. From that place, she sent the note of warning that Sir Henry received. Stapleton stole one of Sir Henry's boots from the hotel, in order to acquaint the hound with his scent. But when Stapleton discovered that the first boot was too new to carry any personal scent, he had to steal an older one. It was the robbery of this second boot that initially convinced Holmes that they were indeed dealing with a real hound.

Partially because of how cleverly Stapleton eluded him while in London, Holmes believes that the man's criminal past was greater than they know. He cites four unsolved burglaries in the area around the moor, in one of which a page lost his life after surprising the burglar. Holmes suspects that Stapleton returned to Devonshire only after realizing that Holmes was on the case in London.

Watson then inquires as to how Stapleton took care of the hound while he was away. Holmes speculates that an old manservant took care of it. This man, named Anthony, has since disappeared from Merripit House, and Holmes believes that this man was actually a South American named Antonio.

Holmes then adds that he could smell white jessamine on the warning note that was sent to Sir Henry. From that detail, he immediately suspected the Stapletons, since Dr. Mortimer had not mentioned many other females who lived out on the moor. Knowing he needed to watch Stapleton, but that the culprit would be too cautious if Holmes were out on the moor, Holmes engineered the ruse of sending Watson alone. However, even from his hidden position, Holmes discovered that he could not collect enough evidence to convict Stapleton unless he caught the man red-handed.

Finally, they discuss Miss Stapleton. Both men believe that Sir Henry's turmoil after the incident is due in large part to a broken heart; he actually did love Miss Stapleton. However, his world trip with Dr. Mortimer is proving an excellent salve to his pain. Though he has no proof of her true feelings for Sir Henry, Holmes does know that Miss Stapleton attempted to stop her husband on the night of the murder, which is why he tied her up.

Watson asks two follow-up questions. First, how could Stapleton have known that the hound would kill Sir Henry, especially since the man had no known health problems? Holmes replies that the animal had been starved, and that its savage appearance would certainly have incapacitated Sir Henry's resistance, even if it did not immediately terrify him to death.

Secondly, how was Stapleton going to explain that he was actually a Baskerville after Sir Henry's death, without raising suspicion?

To this question, Holmes admits that he does not know the answer: "The past and the present are within the field of my inquiry, but what a man may do in the future is a hard question to answer" (318). He speculates that Stapleton might have returned to

South America to establish his claim from there, or that he might have taken a disguise in London. Finally, he considers that Stapleton might have used someone else to claim the estate.

Holmes then invites Watson to join him for dinner and a show.

Analysis

In the last chapter, we receive all the details of the case which were not accounted for through the adventure. This is notable because it reveals one responsibility of the detective story: it must tie up *all* loose ends and clues. Many Holmes scholars have tried to re-interpret some of his cases, to prove Sherlock Holmes wrong. Wanting to prevent this and ensure narrative conviction for all his readers, Doyle ensures that the details of his construction are firmly established, along with the final caveat that Holmes cannot tell the future.

This final chapter also frames the detective story as something of a historical genre as well. It functions by revisiting past events, and re-interpreting the details that readers might have missed. Several small details - like the existence and death of a Rodger Baskerville, or Dr. Mortimer's missing dog - are later shown to be important, while others - like the smell on the warning letter - were even outside of Watson's observation. This quality is important because it inspires the reader to never assume he or she has observed everything. Sometimes, a past event will only reveal its meaning in the light of future events.

Of course, what makes *Hound of the Baskervilles* so unique amongst Holmes stories is the quality of its adventure. Chapter XIV serves as an exciting climax, in many ways. First is the way that it brings the central conflict - of rationality versus superstition - to a head. It is fascinating that even Holmes is shocked into paralysis when the hound first appears. No matter the strength of our intellect, we have a tendency to believe our senses, and Holmes is struck dumb by the appearance of a supernatural being. However, it is more than just the savage appearance - of flames and glitter - and the gothic atmosphere - the overwhelming fog - that make the hound terrifying. It is also the mythology, which all the characters have internalized even if they doubt its veracity. In other words, Doyle does not simply write off the power of fear as subservient to the intellect, but rather gives it its due. One of other element of fearful uncertainty is that Stapleton's body is never found - it is entirely possible that he remains alive.

In the end, Doyle obviously comes down on the side of rationality. Even this horrific beast can be rationally understood, its most savage qualities explained. But the idea - that everything has a scientific explanation if one knows how to look - is all the more powerful because it follows such an exciting climax, one that exploits all the atmosphere, gloom and terror of the novel's earlier chapters to engineer a deadly chase. Knowledge is most certainly power, as the novel has made clear, but one has to sometimes transcend one's instinctual fears and superstitions to obtain this knowledge.

Finally, the reader might have some moral qualms about the end of the tale. The criminal has died, and Sir Henry is so traumatized that he must take a year long vacation. A modern reader might find Stapleton's inexorable evil a bit off-putting, since we tend to think any criminal can be reformed. However, as mentioned previously, attitudes on crime in Doyle's day tended to see depravity as an inherent, unfixable problem. Therefore, a criminal must be caught in the act, as Holmes does. The idea of acting proactively - whether through social programs or personal psychology - was simply not something Holmes or Doyle would have explicitly considered.

Suggested Essay Questions

1. **How does Holmes interpret clues? How is this different from how others approach clues?**

   Holmes is unique because he is capable of seeing unusual meanings for everyday objects. He looks to see what they might mean to someone else, rather than simply assuming that they only signify one thing. For example, whereas everyone else assumes that Sir Henry's boots go missing because an employee was incompetent, Holmes uses this seemingly insignificant detail to deduce that there is actually a hound involved. He imagines other possibilities. In other cases, Holmes looks for the markers humans have left on objects. An example of this would be the warning letter sent to Sir Henry; Holmes uses marks on it to deduce what newspaper it came from and that it was written by a woman. Overall, Holmes refuses to make assumptions, but rather considers what else any object can show to the discerning observer.
2. **How does Holmes use his imagination to solve crime? Use a specific example, and also contrast this use of the imagination to that of Watson.**

   Holmes uses his imagination insofar as he conceives of more than one interpretation for any apparent fact. For example, he is the only one who pieces together that Stapleton and Miss Stapleton are actually married; though there was no explicit evidence of this connection, Holmes is willing to consider different explanations than simply the one they provide. Because he can imagine these possibilities, he is better able to deduce how various clues work together. Watson, on the other hand, is what Holmes call "a man of action." Though he is hardly a fool, he is less able to make imaginative leaps. For instance, when he observes Stapleton's intense opposition to a match between Sir Henry and Miss Stapleton, Watson acknowledges an oddity but does not consider seemingly bizarre possibilities, and hence does not discover what Holmes does.
3. **What is the effect and purpose of Watson's narration?**

   Watson is important as a narrator for several reasons. First, as an intelligent man who can nevertheless come nowhere close to replicating Holmes's method, he provides even the clever reader a lens through which to appreciate Holmes's singular genius. Furthermore, Holmes remains distant and mysterious largely because he does not narrate his own tales. Holmes only shares his final process with Watson, which keeps many particulars of his imaginative method attractively ambiguous. Finally, in this novel in particular, Doyle is able to explore the case in two literal ways at once, by having Watson travel to Devonshire alone even while Holmes is secretly working in the background.

4. **How would you characterize the relationship between Watson and Holmes.**

   Though ostensibly partners, Watson and Holmes have a much more multi-faceted relationship. Watson admires Holmes, and clearly yearns for the detective's approval. He is more than willing to do what Holmes asks of him, whether it be deducing facts about Dr. Mortimer from the walking stick, or traveling ahead to Devonshire. However, Holmes continues to treat Watson like a subordinate, most obviously when he does not reveal his true plan to Watson until the latter finds him out on the moor. Though Watson acknowledges this ill-treatment, his concerns are quickly quashed, suggesting overall not only that Holmes sees Watson as something of a student, but that Watson sees Holmes as more of a mentor than as a partner.
5. **What does this novel say about untrustworthy eyewitnesses?**

   Most of the untrustworthy eyewitnesses in *The Hound of the Baskervilles* fail not because of ill intent, but because they let their emotions cloud their judgment. For instance, two of the novel's most trustworthy figures - Dr. Mortimer and Dr. Watson - are expected to be impartial observers of the events on the moor. As men of science, they should conceivably not fall prey to the anxieties produced by the old legend. However, both men eventually consider the legend as an explanation for events they cannot otherwise explain, largely because the atmosphere of the moor is so spooky. Therefore, the novel suggests that being a reasonable or honest man does not make one's observations trustworthy. Instead, an eyewitness can only be trusted if he is able to observe facts in themselves, not letting his emotional perspective interfere.
6. **How does the novel explore the conflict between rationalism and the occult?**

   Arguably, this novel's case interests Holmes because it seems to so strongly suggest an occult explanation. Thus, it poses him a challenge: find a rational explanation for what would otherwise be attributed to the supernatural. Throughout the story, characters battle these two opposing forces. The hound is representative of a superstitious belief in evil. Even men of science - Dr. Mortimer and Dr. Watson - somewhat accept the occult explanations, both because they can find no scientific clues to the contrary and because the atmosphere of the moor evokes such conjectures. It is telling that Holmes, by remaining firmly convinced that there must be a rational explanation, eventually discovers that explanation, and even reveals what Stapleton did to make the hound seem so other-worldly. Thus, the novel overall reveals how humans have a tendency towards supernatural explanations, but suggests that we can remain firmly embedded in the rational if we have the strength of will to do so.
7. **How is criminality portrayed in this novel?**

In general, criminals are portrayed as inherently vicious in *The Hound of the Baskervilles*. There is not much suggestion that they can be reformed, which might seem a strange attitude for the modern reader. For instance, Selden is presented as a uniformly bad person. When Watson sees him, he describes the convict's face as resembling an animal. Even Mrs. Barrymore believes her brother is beyond reform. Further, Stapleton's evil is considered "hereditary," passed down from Hugo Baskerville. Though Doyle does give small indications that perhaps there are other approaches to criminality, his general assumption seems to align with that of his day: criminals are simply bad.

8. **What is the significance of Dr. Mortimer's walking stick?**

   This object, the discussion of which comprises much of the first chapter, establishes many of the novel's themes. First, it allows Holmes to introduce the reader to his method of deduction, which is based on the assumption that humans leaves marks behind wherever they go. Secondly, it creates an important contrast between Watson and Holmes. Though Watson does well in examining the stick, Holmes easily outwits him with his own deduction. Though Watson has known Holmes for a long time, he remains unable to intuit like the detective can. Finally, it creates the novel's first suspenseful question: who is this Dr. Mortimer from the country, and what does he want from Holmes?

9. **How does the law play into the story?**

   Though the issue of criminality is central to the entire story, it is only at the end of the novel that Holmes relies on actual legal action. This reticence to involve the law indicates several things. First, law requires firm evidence, not simply Holmes's brilliant deductions. Thus, Holmes has to wait until he can find firm proof of theories he has already proven to himself. Secondly, the delay suggests a certain ineptness on the law's part. The law cannot really catch a criminal until he has already committed his crime. The law's seeming inability or unwillingness to use methods like Holmes's means that it is always behind the ball. In this case, Holmes has to put Sir Henry in danger in order to prove his theory, suggesting that the official law faces a stumbling block towards protecting citizens.

10. **How does city life contrast with country life in this novel, especially in terms of solving crimes?**

    Overall, the novel makes a clear distinction between city and country life: whereas the former allows for a rational mindset in the midst of a bustling populace, the latter evokes more supernatural beliefs because of the solitude. This distinction is also reflected in the way each locale affects crime-solving. The city's advantages involve the networks and directories which Holmes systematically uses to catch criminals. For example, he is easily able to track down the cab driver who was driving the bearded man, and can easily check the nearby hotels for evidence of Miss Stapleton's letter.

However, Holmes moves the investigation to the moor precisely because there are fewer people, and less suspicions of wrongdoing. Because most people there accept the hound legend as somewhat true, he can more easily observe their behaviors and narrow down his suspects. However, country networks are informal, and hence more difficult to explore. For instance, Watson only finds Laura Lyons because Barrymore helps him.

The clever adaptation of BBC's "Sherlock"

There have been many adaptations of the Sherlock Holmes stories over the years, many of which are quite unique or anachronistic. However, one of the most recent, innovative and successful of these adaptations is the BBC show *Sherlock*, starring Benedict Cumberbatch as Sherlock Holmes and Martin Freeman as Doctor John Watson. Set in contemporary London but maintaing much of the atmosphere and approach of Doyle's original stories, the series has proved a massive hit.

Perhaps most interesting is the way the series uses Doyle's original material in updated ways. In episode 2 of season 2, the show adapted *The Hound of the Baskervilles*, in a story about the the possible existence of a spectral hound that haunts a small town. In this telling, the beast is believed to be the product of a government experiment. Throughout the investigation, even Sherlock is led to consider its existence. Ultimately, the hound's terrible appearance is found to be the product of a chemical gas. Interestingly, the story uses the same conflicts - fear of the unknown, the distinction between city and country life - in a contemporary way. People are less afraid of supernatural causes, and more afraid of scientific experiment in a post-atomic age.

Author of ClassicNote and Sources

Mae Ng, author of ClassicNote. Completed on October 30, 2013, copyright held by GradeSaver.

Updated and revised S.R. Cedars February 24, 2013. Copyright held by GradeSaver.

Nordon, Pierre. Conan Doyle: A Biography. New York: Holt, Rinehart, and Winston, 1967.

Hodgson, John A.. Sherlock Holmes: The Major Stories with Contemporary Critical Essays. Boston: Bedford Books of St. Martin's Press, 1994.

Brooks, Peter. Reading for the Plot. New York: A.A. Knopf, 1984.

Todorov, Tzvetan. Poetics of Prose. Ithaca: Cornell University Press, 1977.

Baggett, David, ed. and Philip Tallon, ed.. The Philosophy of Sherlock Holmes. Lexington: University of Kentucky Press, 2012.

Hall, Trevor, ed. Sherlock Holmes: Ten Literary Studies. London: Gerald Duckworth & Co., Ltd., 1969.

Doyle, Sir Arthur Conan. The Complete Sherlock Holmes: Volume II. Garden City, New York: Doubleday, Doran & Company, 1930.

Essay: Significance of Setting in The Hound of the Baskervilles

by Christian Caron
February 25, 2013

In Sir Arthur Conan Doyle's The Hound of the Baskervilles (HOB), Sherlock Holmes and Dr. Watson are immersed in a setting that appears to transcend the known limits of the physical world. A demoniacal hound roaming the moors of Devonshire is rumored to have been responsible for the death of the affluent Sir Charles Baskerville. Dr. Mortimer, a family friend, is left no choice but to recruit the renowned detective and his partner to investigate the case. The narrative, recounted through Dr. Watson's perspective, soon abandons the familiarity of Baker Street in exchange for the ghastliness of Baskerville Hall and its vicinity. Upon Watson's arrival, Dartmoor proves to be every bit as ominous as it was hyped up to be. Sir Arthur Conan Doyle uses the valuable tool of location throughout to leave open the possibility that there are crimes beyond the scope of rational analysis.

The setting first asserts itself when, in the midst of presenting the details of the case to Holmes, Dr. Mortimer reads aloud the myth of the Baskerville curse. One could have easily mistaken the piece for an excerpt from a Gothic novel, for it is ridden with the genre's elements. The reader learns Hugo Baskerville of Baskerville Manor ruthlessly abducted the daughter of a yeoman. After she attempted to escape from the chamber upstairs one night, Baskerville and others chased her onto the moor. Eventually, she and Hugo were both found dead. Beside the body of the latter was, to the astonishment of the other men, "a great, black beast, shaped like a hound, yet larger than any hound that ever mortal eye has rested upon" (Doyle 9). The linkage between the plot and setting of the myth is important. As mentioned, they are both rooted in Gothic tradition and thus play off each other. The somber estate and the damsel in distress are both common elements of Gothic fiction. The degree to which Baskerville is alleged to have been infatuated with her is also indicative of the genre. Furthermore, the hound that lurks at night and the dark moor it inhabits are intentionally portrayed as demonic and supernatural, inviting the possibility that the "Father of Evil" may very well be Sir Charles' assailant. Holmes—the embodiment of the Enlightenment—is, notably, more skeptical than the others, but even he does not completely rule out the chance that "forces outside the ordinary laws of Nature" may be at work (19). Additionally, the gloomy, Gothic setting established in the exposition matches the description Watson later gives of Dartmoor when he and Sir Charles actually arrive there. Suddenly, it seems less likely that the mystery is capable of being solved in the physical world through deductive reasoning.

The great Grimpen Mire, capable of sinking one in its depths, evolves into a grisly metaphor for the mystery itself. Not coincidentally, it is navigable only by the naturalist Mr. Stapleton—the perpetrator of the crime—and eventually found to be the location of the hound's fortress. Watson, after observing the mire's capabilities, says, "Life has become like that great Grimpen Mire, with little green patches everywhere into which one may sink and with no guide to point the track" (54). This comparison expresses the imminent danger and apparent hopelessness of their predicament, which contributes to the suspense of the Gothic atmosphere. It also portrays Watson as an ill-equipped assistant in the absence of Holmes' analytical mind. One could imagine that Doyle added in this additional component specifically to evoke despair. How will Watson alone—a mere mortal—be able to solve a murder as complex as this one?

The presumption that the case is ultimately out of Holmes' and Watson's control again seems feasible toward the end of the story, when a blinding fog threatens the plan the former had concocted to lure the hound out onto the moor. Using Sir Henry—the heir to Baskerville Hall—as bait, Holmes, Watson, and Lestrade wait anxiously behind a series of rocks for the hound to appear. When the fog begins to engulf the moor, Holmes observes, "If he isn't out in a quarter of an hour the path will be covered. In half an hour we won't be able to see our hands in front of us" (111). Fog has traditionally been interpreted as a metaphor for confusion. If it had prevented the hound from being caught, the beast's nature and other pertinent information would also remain clouded. But perhaps just as importantly, Sir Henry would almost certainly meet his doom if no one could get a clear shot on the hound. This adds yet another Gothic twist to the climax, and the case—for one last time—seems as if it may be out of Holmes' grasp.

HOB deviates from the typical Sherlock Holmes mystery. Setting is imperative in creating the illusion of a world that would render even the elite detective powerless. As later affirmed, however, a supernatural world is merely a world not yet understood. Though complex, the physical world—at its core—is an orderly, comprehensible place if analyzed rationally. The eventual unmasking of Stapleton and demystification of the hound are testaments to this. But before that happens, the reader is, albeit temporarily, fooled into thinking HOB is a full-fledged Gothic novel. For the sake of creating a believable work, Sir Arthur Conan Doyle abandons this, just as Holmes and Watson return to a natural explanation for phenomena after shortly contemplating a supernatural one.

Quiz 1

1. **Holmes is described as _________.**
   A. an early riser
   B. slovenly
   C. a late riser
   D. well-groomed

2. **At the beginning of the novel, Holmes sees Watson through __________.**
   A. a mirror
   B. binoculars
   C. a silver coffee pot
   D. a reflective glass window

3. **What hotel does Sir Henry stay at?**
   A. Northumberland Hotel
   B. Greenwich Hotel
   C. London Hotel
   D. Charing Cross Hotel

4. **What is stolen from Sir Henry's hotel?**
   A. a cigar
   B. a letter
   C. a newspaper
   D. a boot

5. **To the cab driver, who does the mystery man claim he is?**
   A. Sir Henry
   B. Sherlock Holmes
   C. Dr. Mortimer
   D. John Watson

6. **What object does Watson bring with him to Devonshire?**
   A. a hat
   B. a map
   C. a gun
   D. a telescope

7. **Who does NOT inherit money immediately upon Sir Charles's death?**
   A. Mrs. Barrymore
   B. Dr. Mortimer
   C. Mr. Barrymore
   D. Rodger Baskerville

8. **What does Holmes ask Cartwright to do in London?**
   A. visit hotels
   B. track down a cab driver
   C. sell newspapers
   D. follow a man

9. **What does CCH stand for?**
   A. Charing Cross Hospital
   B. Club Chestnut Hunt
   C. Charing Cross Hotel
   D. Chesnut Cross Hotel

10. **Which of the following adjectives does NOT describe Dr. Mortimer?**
   A. careless
   B. friendly
   C. slovenly
   D. old

11. **Holmes send a telegram to Baskerville Hall asking after _______.**
   A. Miss Stapleton
   B. Sir Henry
   C. Barrymore
   D. Stapleton

12. **Which of the following details is NOT included in the newspaper clipping that Dr. Mortimer provides?**
   A. Sir Charles was found by Barrymore.
   B. Sir Charles is related to Hugo Baskerville.
   C. Sir Charles was a smoker.
   D. Sir Charles is generous with his money.

13. **When Watson returns from his club in London, what does Holmes show him?**
    A. a newspaper clipping
    B. a map
    C. a man watching them outside the window
    D. a will

14. **Which term best describes Sir Henry's personality?**
    A. mean-spirited
    B. kind
    C. indecisive
    D. hot-tempered

15. **Who witnesses Sir Charles's death?**
    A. Mrs. Barrymore
    B. Murphy, a gipsy horse-dealer
    C. Sir Henry
    D. Mr. Stapleton

16. **What is Dr. Mortimer's special interest?**
    A. skulls
    B. bees
    C. roses
    D. butterflies

17. **Which of the following details is NOT included in the manuscript about the hound?**
    A. Hugo's body was found in a goyal.
    B. It was not Hugo's idea to set the hounds on the maiden.
    C. The maiden's throat was torn out by the hound.
    D. Hugo Baskerville swore his soul to the powers of evil.

18. **What is the newspaper's interpretation of Sir Charles's death?**
    A. He died of an organic disease.
    B. They refuse to offer one.
    C. He died after an attack by a hound.
    D. He died from a fever.

19. **Where was Sir Henry living before he returns to England?**
    A. New York
    B. Germany
    C. Spain
    D. Canada

20. **Which of the following comments does Sir Henry make upon his arrival on the moor?**
    A. He hears a hound.
    B. He will install streetlights.
    C. He likes the trees.
    D. He does not like the towers on the house.

21. **From the warning note sent to Sir Henry, Holmes deduces that the writer is __________.**
    A. a smoker
    B. educated
    C. slovenly
    D. following Sir Henry

22. **What year was the manuscript about the hound written?**
    A. 1650
    B. 1687
    C. 1730
    D. 1742

23. **What county is Baskerville Hall located in?**
    A. Sussex
    B. Yorkshire
    C. Buckingham
    D. Devonshire

24. **Why does the writer of the manuscript want to commit the legend of the hound to paper?**
    A. He believes more knowledge makes one less afraid.
    B. He wants to publicize the dangers of the moor.
    C. He is afraid the legend will be forgotten.
    D. He wants the mystery of the hound solved.

25. **What makes Dr. Mortimer believe in the existence of the hound?**

A. The manuscript proves the existence.

B. He heard the hound.

C. He saw footprints.

D. He found large hairs.

Quiz 1 Answer Key

1. **(C)** a late riser
2. **(C)** a silver coffee pot
3. **(A)** Northumberland Hotel
4. **(D)** a boot
5. **(B)** Sherlock Holmes
6. **(C)** a gun
7. **(D)** Rodger Baskerville
8. **(A)** visit hotels
9. **(A)** Charing Cross Hospital
10. **(D)** old
11. **(C)** Barrymore
12. **(B)** Sir Charles is related to Hugo Baskerville.
13. **(B)** a map
14. **(D)** hot-tempered
15. **(B)** Murphy, a gipsy horse-dealer
16. **(A)** skulls
17. **(C)** The maiden's throat was torn out by the hound.
18. **(A)** He died of an organic disease.
19. **(D)** Canada
20. **(B)** He will install streetlights.
21. **(B)** educated
22. **(D)** 1742
23. **(D)** Devonshire
24. **(A)** He believes more knowledge makes one less afraid.
25. **(C)** He saw footprints.

Quiz 2

1. **Who is NOT on Holmes's suspect list at the time Watson leaves London?**
   A. James Desmond
   B. Stapleton
   C. Dr. Mortimer
   D. Mr. Frankland

2. **Holmes learn about Sir Charles's inheritance money from ________.**
   A. public records
   B. Sir Henry
   C. Dr. Mortimer
   D. a will

3. **What detail does Dr. Mortimer notice in the yew alley?**
   A. a wallet
   B. cigar ashes
   C. the weather
   D. the open hedge-gate

4. **What kind of dog does Dr. Mortimer have?**
   A. poodle
   B. mastiff
   C. spaniel
   D. terrier

5. **How is Sir Henry related to Sir Charles?**
   A. nephew
   B. cousin
   C. brother-in-law
   D. son

6. **Who does Watson unexpectedly meet on his way to Baskerville Hall?**
   A. Selden
   B. Perkins, a guard
   C. Laura Lyons
   D. Mr. Frankland

7. **How is Laura Lyons related to Mr. Frankland?**
   A. cousin
   B. sister
   C. daughter
   D. mistress

8. **Where does Laura Lyons live?**
   A. Coombe Tracey
   B. Sussex
   C. Merripit House
   D. Yorkshire

9. **What is Mr. Stapleton's hobby?**
   A. cigars
   B. cats
   C. guns
   D. butterflies

10. **Who is the detective who comes to Holmes's aid?**
   A. Dickens
   B. Lestrade
   C. Barrymore
   D. Miles

11. **Why does Holmes send Cartwright back to London on the evening of the hound attack?**
   A. He has forgotten his walking stick.
   B. He wants to send him to safety.
   C. He wants Stapleton to believe he is in London.
   D. He wants Cartwright to search the hotels again.

12. **What other name have the Stapletons used?**
   A. Vannison
   B. Van Dc Kamp
   C. Vandeleur
   D. Vandeveter

13. **How is Sir Henry related to Mr. Stapleton?**
   A. nephew
   B. cousin
   C. brother
   D. son

14. **Where does the bulk of Sir Charles's money come from?**
   A. South African speculation
   B. government corruption
   C. Baskerville inheritance
   D. West Indies trading

15. **What is Mrs. Barrymore's relation to the convict on the moor?**
   A. mother
   B. cousin
   C. sister
   D. daughter

16. **Watson is confused to see Barrymore ________.**
   A. burn letters
   B. talk in his sleep
   C. shine a light from an empty room
   D. beat his wife

17. **Laura Lyons wrote Sir Charles to _________.**
   A. warn him
   B. tell him the truth about her husband
   C. arrange a meeting
   D. complain about her father

18. **What is Mr. Frankland's hobby?**
   A. skulls
   B. kidnapping dogs
   C. lawsuits
   D. butterflies

19. **Watson find Holmes in Devonshire __________.**

A. with the help of Laura Lyons

B. with the help of Mr. Frankland

C. by following Mr. Stapleton

D. on his search for Dr. Mortimer's dog

20. **Why is Miss Stapleton not present at dinner on the night of the attack?**

A. She has run away.

B. She is sick.

C. She has been killed.

D. She has been tied up.

21. **Which of the following written forms is NOT used in the narration?**

A. telegram

B. manuscript

C. diary entry

D. newspaper article

22. **Why does Holmes keep his presence on the moor a secret from Watson?**

A. He distrusts Watson.

B. He needs to do his own work, undetected.

C. He wants to encourage Watson's own detective skills.

D. He was too distracted to tell him.

23. **Barrymore tells Watson a secret about _________.**

A. Sir Charles's spying habits

B. the letter from Laura Lyons

C. the hound

D. a tweed suit

24. **How does Holmes surprise Laura Lyons?**

A. by jumping out of the bushes

B. by lying to her

C. by telling her that Mr. Frankland is not her father

D. by telling her that Mr. Stapleton is married

25. **What does Watson see when he follows Sir Henry out on to the moor?**
   A. a hound
   B. Sherlock Holmes
   C. a meeting with Beryl Stapleton
   D. a meeting with Dr. Mortimer

Quiz 2 Answer Key

1. **(A)** James Desmond
2. **(C)** Dr. Mortimer
3. **(B)** cigar ashes
4. **(C)** spaniel
5. **(A)** nephew
6. **(B)** Perkins, a guard
7. **(C)** daughter
8. **(A)** Coombe Tracey
9. **(D)** butterflies
10. **(B)** Lestrade
11. **(C)** He wants Stapleton to believe he is in London.
12. **(C)** Vandeleur
13. **(B)** cousin
14. **(A)** South African speculation
15. **(C)** sister
16. **(C)** shine a light from an empty room
17. **(C)** arrange a meeting
18. **(C)** lawsuits
19. **(B)** with the help of Mr. Frankland
20. **(D)** She has been tied up.
21. **(D)** newspaper article
22. **(B)** He needs to do his own work, undetected.
23. **(B)** the letter from Laura Lyons
24. **(D)** by telling her that Mr. Stapleton is married
25. **(C)** a meeting with Beryl Stapleton

Quiz 3

1. **What is the name of the cab driver?**
   A. John Berrymore
   B. Henry Mann
   C. John Clayton
   D. Henry Aspern

2. **When was this novel written?**
   A. 1893
   B. 1898
   C. 1899
   D. 1901

3. **What journal published this novel?**
   A. Strand
   B. London Review
   C. Ford
   D. Times

4. **How does Holmes know Cartwright?**
   A. through Watson
   B. He found him on the street.
   C. He is related to him.
   D. through Dr. Mortimer

5. **What does Sir Charles suffer from?**
   A. a nervous condition
   B. paranoia
   C. migraines
   D. depression

6. **Why does Dr. Mortimer withhold information from the newspaper?**
   A. He doesn't want to encourage rumors.
   B. He isn't sure he saw a paw print.
   C. He has murdered Sir Charles.
   D. He doesn't want to ruin Sir Charles's reputation.

7. **Where does Sir Charles die?**
   A. in Grimpen Mire
   B. an alley
   C. inside the house
   D. in the goyal

8. **What is Miss Stapleton's first name?**
   A. Cheryl
   B. Joan
   C. Alice
   D. Beryl

9. **Who took care of the hound in Mr Stapleton's absence?**
   A. a manservant, Anthony
   B. Miss Stapleton
   C. Cartwright
   D. nobody; the hound nearly starved

10. **What is Mr. Stapleton's former occupation?**
   A. sailor
   B. mathematician
   C. schoolteacher
   D. detective

11. **How many brothers did Sir Charles have?**
   A. one
   B. two
   C. none
   D. three

12. **Which of the following locations is NOT mentioned in the novel?**
   A. Coombe Tracey
   B. London
   C. Sussex
   D. Devonshire

13. **What does Holmes smell on the warning letter?**
    A. vanilla
    B. white jessamine
    C. tea tree oil
    D. sweet orange

14. **Which of the following words does NOT describe Selden?**
    A. savage
    B. crafty
    C. yellow
    D. amusing

15. **How many men witness Hugo Baskerville's death, according to the legend?**
    A. one
    B. two
    C. four
    D. three

16. **How does the newspaper describe Sir Charles's footprints the night of his death?**
    A. tip-toe
    B. disappearing
    C. running
    D. half-sunken

17. **Where do the Stapletons live?**
    A. Merripit House
    B. Coombe House
    C. Tracey House
    D. Merriweather House

18. **What does Watson hear on his first night at Baskerville Hall?**
    A. a hound
    B. Mr. Barrymore's footsteps
    C. a loud thump
    D. a woman's cry

19. **What does Watson do when Holmes is thinking alone about the case?**
   A. He obtains a map at city hall.
   B. He researches in the library.
   C. He goes to his club.
   D. He follows Sir Henry.

20. **Who narrates the story?**
   A. Holmes
   B. Watson
   C. Dr. Mortimer
   D. Lyons

21. **What does Selden do when he sees Watson and Sir Henry?**
   A. He hides.
   B. He hurls rocks at them.
   C. He shoots at them.
   D. He screams.

22. **Why does Laura Lyons keep her letter to Sir Charles a secret?**
   A. She is afraid she'll be blamed for his death.
   B. Miss Stapleton tells her to.
   C. Her husband has frightened her.
   D. She does not want to ruin her reputation.

23. **How does Watson trick Frankland into telling him more about the man on the moor?**
   A. He writes him a letter.
   B. He feigns disinterest.
   C. He tells him about his daughter.
   D. He interrogates him.

24. **Why do Holmes and Watson believe Selden is Sir Henry?**
   A. They hear from Dr. Mortimer that Sir Henry has died.
   B. Selden is wearing Henry's tweed suit.
   C. They recognize Henry's scream.
   D. Selden is wearing Henry's boots.

25. **Who do Watson and Holmes meet over Selden's body?**

A. Sir Henry
B. Mortimer
C. Frankland
D. Stapleton

Quiz 3 Answer Key

1. **(C)** John Clayton
2. **(D)** 1901
3. **(A)** Strand
4. **(A)** through Watson
5. **(A)** a nervous condition
6. **(A)** He doesn't want to encourage rumors.
7. **(B)** an alley
8. **(D)** Beryl
9. **(A)** a manservant, Anthony
10. **(C)** schoolteacher
11. **(B)** two
12. **(C)** Sussex
13. **(B)** white jessamine
14. **(D)** amusing
15. **(D)** three
16. **(A)** tip-toe
17. **(A)** Merripit House
18. **(D)** a woman's cry
19. **(C)** He goes to his club.
20. **(C)** Dr. Mortimer
21. **(B)** He hurls rocks at them.
22. **(A)** She is afraid she'll be blamed for his death.
23. **(B)** He feigns disinterest.
24. **(B)** Selden is wearing Henry's tweed suit.
25. **(D)** Stapleton

Quiz 4

1. **How does Holmes discover Stapleton's motive for his crime?**
   A. He follows Stapleton.
   B. He researches in the library.
   C. He sees a portrait in Baskerville Hall.
   D. He threatens Laura Lyons.

2. **The hound is a breed of _________.**
   A. pitbull and mastiff
   B. mastiff and german shepherd
   C. mastiff and bloodhound
   D. pitbull and bloodhound

3. **What does Sir Henry do after the attack?**
   A. moves to London
   B. sails to America
   C. takes a year long trip around the world
   D. resumes his uncle's charity work

4. **The hound is made more frightening by __________.**
   A. a trick with mirrors
   B. steroids
   C. fake teeth
   D. phosphorus on his mouth

5. **Which of the following is NOT characteristic of the place where Sir Charles died?**
   A. entrance to Baskerville Hall
   B. six foot long strips of grass
   C. hedge-gate
   D. roses

6. **What is Holmes's attitude toward his opponent?**
   A. respect
   B. confusion
   C. hate
   D. disinterest

7. **Where does Selden escape from?**
   A. Sussex
   B. Chestnut Insane Asylum
   C. Derbyville
   D. Princetown

8. **How does Watson fare in Holmes's absence?**
   A. He wishes for Holmes' arrival.
   B. He is able to solve where the hound is located.
   C. He is able to figure out that Stapleton is a criminal.
   D. He always accompanies Sir Henry.

9. **Sir Henry threatens to ________ Mr. Barrymore.**
   A. report
   B. fire
   C. kill
   D. ruin

10. **How does the maiden escape from Hugo Baskerville?**
    A. She jumps out the window, breaking her leg.
    B. She climbs down a rope.
    C. She sneaks past the carousing party.
    D. She climbs down ivy-covered walls.

11. **Which of the following words is used to describe Stapleton?**
    A. connoisseur
    B. intellectual
    C. hobbyist
    D. naturalist

12. **Watson describes the people on the moor as ________.**
    A. gypsies
    B. primitive
    C. law and order types
    D. empty

13. **What month does this novel take place in?**
    A. August
    B. October
    C. January
    D. April

14. **How does Watson learn the identity of L.L?**
    A. Stapleton tells him.
    B. He looks it up in a directory.
    C. Dr. Mortimer tells him.
    D. Frankland tells him.

15. **What does Watson see through Frankland's telescope?**
    A. Sir Henry's argument with Stapleton
    B. a man on the moor
    C. a child delivering food
    D. the convict

16. **How does Holmes recognize the source of the warning letter?**
    A. its ink
    B. a fingerprint
    C. a smudge in the corner
    D. its typescript

17. **Who shoots the hound?**
    A. Holmes
    B. Watson
    C. Lestrade
    D. Sir Henry

18. **Which of the following does NOT describe Hugo Baskerville?**
    A. clever
    B. profane
    C. godless
    D. wild

19. **How does Holmes respond to Dr. Mortimer's manuscript?**
   A. He makes some deductions about its writer.
   B. He is interested in the science of it.
   C. He calls it a fairytale.
   D. He believes Hugo is a bad person.

20. **How does Stapleton explain the howling sound on the moor?**
   A. He says it is Dr. Mortimer's dog.
   B. He thinks it is the wind.
   C. He says it is a bird.
   D. He believes in the legend.

21. **How does Holmes find out that the Stapletons are married?**
   A. He researches the school they once owned.
   B. He meets someone who once knew them.
   C. He spies on them in their house.
   D. He overhears a conversation they are having.

22. **Where was Stapleton born?**
   A. South America
   B. England
   C. South Africa
   D. Canada

23. **Who employs a disguise in this novel?**
   A. Holmes
   B. Watson
   C. Stapleton
   D. Cartwright

24. **Why does Miss Stapleton warn Watson to leave the moor?**
   A. She knows he will find out the truth.
   B. She is afraid of him.
   C. She believes he is Sir Henry.
   D. She believes he is Sherlock Holmes.

25. **After inquiring about the cab driver, Holmes and Watson spend two hours _________.**
    A. eating dinner
    B. researching the moor
    C. arguing
    D. in a museum

Quiz 4 Answer Key

1. **(C)** He sees a portrait in Baskerville Hall.
2. **(C)** mastiff and bloodhound
3. **(C)** takes a year long trip around the world
4. **(D)** phosphorus on his mouth
5. **(D)** roses
6. **(A)** respect
7. **(D)** Princetown
8. **(A)** He wishes for Holmes' arrival.
9. **(B)** fire
10. **(D)** She climbs down ivy-covered walls.
11. **(D)** naturalist
12. **(B)** primitive
13. **(B)** October
14. **(C)** Dr. Mortimer tells him.
15. **(C)** a child delivering food
16. **(D)** its typescript
17. **(A)** Holmes
18. **(A)** clever
19. **(C)** He calls it a fairytale.
20. **(C)** He says it is a bird.
21. **(A)** He researches the school they once owned.
22. **(A)** South America
23. **(C)** Stapleton
24. **(C)** She believes he is Sir Henry.
25. **(D)** in a museum

ClassicNotes

GradeSaver™

Getting you the grade since 1999™

Other ClassicNotes from GradeSaver™

A Farewell to Arms
The Federalist Papers
Fences
Fight Club
Fight Club (Film)
Flags of Our Fathers
Flannery O'Connor's Stories
Flight
For Colored Girls Who Have Considered Suicide When the Rainbow Is Enuf
For Whom the Bell Tolls
Founding Brothers
The Fountainhead
Frankenstein
Franny and Zooey
The Giver
The Glass Castle
The Glass Menagerie
The God of Small Things
The Godfather
Goethe's Faust
The Good Earth
The Good Woman of Setzuan
Gorilla, My Love
The Grapes of Wrath
Great Expectations
The Great Gatsby
Grendel
The Guest
Gulliver's Travels
Hamlet
The Handmaid's Tale
Hard Times
Haroun and the Sea of Stories
Harry Potter and the Philosopher's Stone
Heart of Darkness
Hedda Gabler
Henry IV (Pirandello)
Henry IV Part 1
Henry IV Part 2
Henry V
Herzog
Hippolytus
The History of Tom Jones, a Foundling
The Hobbit
Homo Faber
The Hound of the Baskervilles
The House of Bernarda Alba
House of Mirth
The House of the Seven Gables
The House of the Spirits
House on Mango Street
How the Garcia Girls Lost Their Accents
Howards End
A Hunger Artist
The Hunger Games
I Know Why the Caged Bird Sings
I, Claudius
An Ideal Husband
Iliad
The Importance of Being Earnest
In Cold Blood
In Our Time
In the Skin of a Lion
In the Time of the Butterflies
Incidents in the Life of a Slave Girl
Inherit the Wind
An Inspector Calls
Interpreter of Maladies
Into the Wild
Invisible Man
Ishmael
The Island of Dr. Moreau
Island of the Blue Dolphins
Jane Eyre
Jazz
The Jew of Malta
Johnny Tremain
Joseph Andrews
A Journal of the Plague Year
The Joy Luck Club
Jude the Obscure
Julius Caesar
The Jungle
Jungle of Cities
Kama Sutra
Kate Chopin's Short Stories
Kidnapped
King Lear
King Solomon's Mines

ClassicNotes

GradeSaver™

Getting you the grade since 1999™

Other ClassicNotes from GradeSaver™

Never Let Me Go
New Introductory Lectures on Psychoanalysis
Nickel and Dimed: On (Not) Getting By in America
Night
Nine Stories
No Exit
North and South
Northanger Abbey
Notes from Underground
Number the Stars
O Pioneers
The Odyssey
Oedipus Rex or Oedipus the King
Of Mice and Men
The Old Man and the Sea
Oliver Twist
On Liberty
On the Road
One Day in the Life of Ivan Denisovich
One Flew Over the Cuckoo's Nest
One Hundred Years of Solitude
Oroonoko
Oryx and Crake
Othello
Our Town
The Outsiders
Pale Fire
Pamela: Or Virtue Rewarded
Paradise Lost
A Passage to India
The Pearl
Pedro Paramo
Percy Shelley: Poems
Perfume: The Story of a Murderer
Persepolis: The Story of a Childhood
Persuasion
Phaedra
Phaedrus
The Piano Lesson
The Picture of Dorian Gray
Pilgrim's Progress
The Playboy of the Western World
Poe's Poetry
Poe's Short Stories
Poems of W.B. Yeats: The Rose
Poems of W.B. Yeats: The Tower
The Poems of William Blake
The Poisonwood Bible
Pope's Poems and Prose
Portrait of the Artist as a Young Man
The Praise of Folly
Pride and Prejudice
The Prince
The Professor's House
Prometheus Bound
Pudd'nhead Wilson
Purple Hibiscus
Pygmalion
Rabbit, Run
A Raisin in the Sun
The Real Life of Sebastian Knight
Rebecca
The Red Badge of Courage
The Remains of the Day
The Republic
Return of the Native
Rhinoceros
Richard II
Richard III
The Rime of the Ancient Mariner
Rip Van Winkle and Other Stories
The Road
Robert Browning: Poems
Robert Frost: Poems
Robinson Crusoe
Roll of Thunder, Hear My Cry
Roman Fever and Other Stories
Romeo and Juliet
A Room of One's Own
A Room With a View
A Rose For Emily and Other Short Stories

For our full list of over 250 Study Guides, Quizzes, Sample College Application Essays, Literature Essays and E-texts, visit:

www.gradesaver.com